THE DIARY OF

A

SHOPKEEPER

STUART WILSON

The Diary Of A Shopkeeper

First Printing - 2015

ISBN:1514866153

Black Bay Publishing

www.BlackBayPublishing.com

CONTENTS

Acknowledgments

To Black Bay Publishing and in particular Ian Yates whose patience knows no bounds. And my heartfelt gratitude for his diligence, determination but above all for his friendship.

To all the people who have shown great interest in this book and for their encouraging and positive words. Thank you.

A special mention to my brother John, my business partner for many years.

And the customers and local community for supporting our independent shop for over 20 years.

And of course to my wife Angie and my daughter Tess. Both so inspirational on a daily basis. And for teaching me how to love.

And to everyone that I should have but did not mention. Thank you

Stuart Wilson
August 2015

One - Mrs Field

The first

Mrs Field, Mrs Evelyn Field was the first ever customer to come through the door.

'Can I buy it now?' were the first words she spoke. Mrs Field was referring to the bottle of whisky she had wanted to buy some days ago.

We had encountered her a few times whilst getting the shop ready for business. She seemed to have a direct aggressive style of communication.

'Bells,' she said, pointing at the whisky. Her hand shook slightly as she pointed, and her fingers were stained with nicotine.

I took the bottle from the shelf and began wrapping it in tissue paper.

'I don't need that,' she said, referring to the wrapping paper, 'or that,' she snapped as I picked up a carrier bag.

Mrs Field had walked into the shop on Monday. The door had been open to air the room as the paint was being touched up on the walls and some of the shelves. She had been told politely that the store was not yet ready, or open for business.

'All I want is that,' she had said, pointing to a case of Bells whisky stacked amongst the other boxes. French wines, beers from Canada and China, local ales, vodka and gin and foreign liqueurs; Mrs Field had spotted the Bells whisky amongst all of this. It had been explained to her that there was no till in place and no change on the premises. In addition to this we were anxious not to fall foul of the law before even beginning to trade.

We felt, perhaps naively that all monies taken should go through the till to be registered. We had no desire to lose our licence before it had been put to proper use.

'I'll leave the correct money then,' she had said, beginning to rifle in her purse. On being refused again, perhaps as much to do with her direct style of communication, as to the lack of a till, Mrs Field conceded defeat and left without the whisky and somewhat surprisingly without speaking another word. Today though she was thanked politely as she paid for her whisky and thanked again as she made to leave the shop. I was pleased we had had our first customer and felt like smiling. Such a small thing yet I was elated as for a while now I had been worried. What if the doors were open for trade and no-one came in. One hour could pass then another and then the first silent empty day and then a week and so on. It had seemed unlikely but not impossible, it hadn't seemed that.

Now there had been a sale and a transaction had been undertaken. Money had been exchanged for product.

'Wasn't so difficult was it?' said Mrs Field smiling now. She was referring, I think, to the fact that it had taken four days, before she was able to buy the whisky, though now her smile seemed more a smile of encouragement than anything else. Perhaps she had sensed that nerves and our desire to do the right thing had influenced our initial response to her and the fear of an empty shop.

I smiled and thanked her one more time. The display panel on the till read seven pounds and ninety nine pence. The shop would not lie empty, a ghostly mausoleum. Its walls lined with bottles of wine, whisky and gin and beers from China and Canada, gathering dust as they sat on the shelves going out of date, unwanted, unsold.

It would seem Mrs Field, Mrs Evelyn Field was right. It wasn't so difficult after all. And seven pounds, ninety nine already in the till.

Two - Sylvia and Peter

A love story - Bogart and Bacall

Even when Sylvia was on her own, as she was today, we would still think of her as Sylvia of Sylvia and Peter. The same applied to Peter on the rare occasions that we would see him without Sylvia, totally synonymous, both names always. One name would leave them incomplete. Two names always, like Bogart and Bacall and Morecombe and Wise, though in fact Hepburn and Tracy would be closer. Sylvia and Peter a trademark, a copyright or a title almost. Sylvia and Peter were wealthy though anything but showy about their financial position. Always buying wines at the lower end of the price scale. She would often, in the course of our brief interactions say things along the lines of 'extravagance is the road to ruin, that route leads to the workhouse' and other such idioms. Although with Sylvia, denial of economic comfort may simply have been modesty. She was not for boasting or ostentatious displays of wealth.

Sylvia wanted to place her usual order, though today there was to be a slight variation. Some new people had moved in a few doors down from them, four doors to be exact. Sylvia liked to be exact, Sylvia was always exact. She also liked to be informed of any changes in the immediate neighbourhood. 'Have you met them?' she asked, 'Have they been in? What do they drink, white wine or red? Sherry perhaps or whisky or beer?' she asked finally, though she hoped it was not beer. Sylvia believed that beer, meaning lager, was not a good thing.

'Turns people queer,' she had said on a previous visit.
A new couple had been in the shop in the last few days,
both in their early sixties. They had mentioned that they
were new to the area. I told Sylvia that they seemed nice
enough and that they were well spoken and polite. Sylvia
seemed pleased to hear this. She was also pleased and I
think relieved that they had purchased wine and not lager.
Red wines, mainly from France or Italy, old world wines.
This too was good for her.

 Sylvia wondered aloud what they did. Sylvia knew what
most people did. It was not intrusiveness on her part, or
nosiness. To her it was a reasonable requirement to be
aware of the goings on in the area where she and Peter
lived their lives. A home to Sylvia was about more than a
building you lived in. It was about the vicinity, the
community and the people who lived in that community.
Sylvia and Peter could list amongst their close personal
friends, magistrates and doctors, lawyers and a high court
judge or two. The Chief of Police also could be added to
their list of friends. Still though they would greet the
postman politely when he brought the mail, the local
paperboy too. He would be offered a glass of squash, or a
coke whenever they encountered him delivering their
Sunday newspapers. A glass of squash, a smile and a brief
chat too.
Sylvia told me, regarding her order, that delivery first
thing in the morning would be 'super', but if I didn't mind
she would take the Bollinger with her now, and perhaps a
bottle of Medoc or St.Emilion. She had received a note
from her new neighbours. She and Peter had been invited
'round for drinks'. The Champagne was for them. And now

that she knew a little more about them, the French wine too.

Three - Charlie

Charlie used to be a landlord

Charlie the lorry driver was content now. Charlie used to be the landlord of one of the big town centre pubs. I knew him from that time. Then he was a typical city centre landlord. Rude and abrupt, confrontational to the point of aggression. And loud, I remember Charlie from that time as being very loud indeed.

Now, when he delivered to us, bringing cases of Stella, cans of Coke and Seven Up, and boxes of crisps, now he was a delight. Softly spoken and humorous, hard-working, patient and gentle. Perhaps most of all gentle. If he was not speaking, he would be whistling or singing softly to and for himself.

'It made me ill in the end,' he told me as he unloaded the goods, 'seven years of dealing with the public in drink, and four of them I was on antidepressants. That can't be right can it?' he asked, passing down the boxes of crisps. I told him that I understood what he meant to a certain degree at least and that no I agreed, it was not right. But Charlie wasn't really listening. He had no real need of confirmation from anyone regarding the difficulty of those years.

Charlie had moved to the rear of the truck now trying to get to the cans of lager buried there. Someone had placed the goods scheduled for a later delivery on top of the ones he needed now and though it meant extra work it didn't seem to bother him. There was no shouting, no aggression shown, simply working quietly to uncover the beers.

Sounds of straining could be heard and of whistling too.

Four - Adele

Adele starts Up

Adele called in today as a customer. Adele works here, works for us or we work for her, sometimes I am unsure which. We inherited Adele with the shop. She had worked with the previous owners for many years. 'Trustworthy and reliable' they had made a point of saying, 'and a good worker too.'

They had asked us to consider keeping her on which we were happy to do. Even then Adele had seemed elderly, her face caked in makeup or powder too pale for her skin. Her lips bright red, contrasted starkly with the face powder. The lipstick applied haphazardly, heavily and often smudged. Her eyes also had not escaped the same severe attention. Pitch black mascara and brightly coloured eye shadow, sometimes lime green or powder blue, even on occasion orange. Perhaps in an effort to match or contrast with the pale skin and the red lipstick; mesmerising to look at, a medieval mask or a pantomime dame. The heart of an angel but a face that would trouble grown men and prey on young children in the night leaving them unsure as to what manner of creature was she, and whether she was a force for good, or a messenger of evil.

She was neither, she was Adele, and today Adele was drunk. Some years ago she had undergone heart surgery. She had 'died' on the operating table more than once, but now though she was alive and animated, dancing to the tune of a cocktail of draught Guinness and prescription drugs.

Adele wasn't a drinker but today was a day off and she 'rather fancied a beer'. She reeled around the shop until she located the Guinness, which she herself had stocked the previous day. She smiled at everyone, staff and customers alike and slurred at anyone game enough to listen to her. Also she planted bright red lipstick strewn kisses on myself and Philip, the young lad helping today. Adele had been out of commission for three months following her heart problems. She was placed under sedation for a period of time by the medical staff following several operations. Her mental condition being they believed, a hazard to her physical recovery. Adele's husband had squandered all of her money in those three months, his own too. Never the most confident of people, Adele was devastated when, with the money gone he left her, and to compound the agony, it was for a younger woman.

Adele had been prescribed sleeping tablets since that time. A poor sleeper, these pills needed to be powerful. They were.

She placed two cans of Guinness on the counter, moving her shoulders from left to right with the music that was playing in the shop. There was a mischievous look in her eye and for a moment I thought she intended to ask one of us to dance with her.

Sometimes she would take one of these tablets if she felt badly in need of a night's sleep, sometimes she wouldn't. The ones unused she would put aside in a jar.

Adele, like many elderly people had an innate fear of becoming a burden. She claimed she would know when that time had come, 'Not now, not yet,' she would say in a matter of fact way before adding mysteriously that, 'It's not that far off either.'

Today Adele was happy partly due to the medication and the stout. But happy all the same as she planted one final kiss on Philips' cheek before departing, to head home with the drinks which she insisted on paying for, to her flat, her empty flat immaculately tidy and spotlessly clean. And somewhere within it a stockpile of sleeping pills sitting in a jar waiting for the day they would be needed when the burden of life finally outweighed its pleasures. Not everyone has the ability to recognise that moment. Adele would though. She would recognise it, acknowledge it and after all her patience and stockpiling, act upon it.

Five - The Drunks

Drunk Y

Drunk Y did a little busking by day. He would keep his evenings free to enable him to begin drinking in earnest. He dressed in a jacket that resembled an American confederate army tunic. With this he wore a cap that almost matched but not quite.

He always seemed cheerful and would laugh and chat freely in the time it took to buy his Special Brews. If he'd had a 'good shift' he would spend a little extra on whisky. This night in late December he was particularly happy as his day had gone well. According to him people were different at this time of the year. Less aggressive, warmer, and perhaps most importantly, far more generous regarding his busking money. There was something though, something even better than this. He had found himself a place to sleep in Broad Street. There was a narrow space between two of the shops and though there was no cover there was a curve that took him out of sight of the people passing on the street. And the walls protected him from the worst of the wind. Still better yet the shops would be closed over much of the festive period enabling him to spend time there in the daytime if he wanted to. To nap for an hour or so, or read a book peacefully and in private.

'Just right, ' he said, 'lovely and so quiet. A lovely little place, really lovely. '

Six - The Choirmaster

The choirmaster

The choirmaster called in often, though never on a daily basis. Some regular drinkers chose to vary their place of purchase, dilute the visibility of their drinking if not the actual amount consumed. Secrecy is often a necessity in the life of a hardened drinker. At times absolutely essential if the drinker is to be able to continue his imbibing unchecked and to his required level. Then sometimes he must be surreptitious to the point of deceit, closed and cunning regarding both the volume and the frequency of consumption. Deceitful to family and friends alike; skilled when covering a trail, adept at lying to prevent any exposure that may result in the curtailing of future availability.

If others acknowledged the extent of his drinking then the assumption would be that he should acknowledge it also, recognise there may be a problem. Therefore he would be expected to drastically reduce the levels of drinking or worse still, be expected to stop altogether. Many serious drinkers found it better to lie rather than cease their drinking. Lie to others when need be and lie to themselves, perhaps especially to themselves.

By chance this day the choirmaster was not in my place of work, I was in his. He was overseeing the choir at a Christmas concert of hymns and carols. He was almost unrecognisable from the pale anxious customer who would purchase seven or eight cans of super strength lager on each visit to the shop. He would be humming tunelessly as he bought his beers, though inside his head, no doubt, would be a heavenly chorus. Pitch perfect and harmonious. His hands would always shake as he made his payment and I felt the humming was partly a device to discourage any social interaction. His mind often seemed to be elsewhere and his nervous system made fragile by alcohol would rather not engage with a virtual stranger. Here in the college chapel though he was different. There was no way of knowing of course if he had taken a drink, though I felt that he had not. As he instructed the choir, baton in hand, he was changed, confident now and assured, in control. In control of the choir, of the music and in control of himself. And something else, something else altogether. As he conducted he was smiling, a joyous smile something I had never seen before, rousing the choir, persuading them, encouraging them to sing, inspiring them to do so. Convincing them that, while they were wonderful, they could be more wonderful still. And so he continued through sections of the Messiah, through hymns and carols. Responsible for filling the small chapel with sounds that would not have been out of place in heaven itself. No amount of alcohol could equal the feeling within him now. He was doing something that he loved and he was good at it too. No drink or drug has yet been created that can surpass that. Nothing really could even come close.

Seven - Gary

Gary and the Nazis

Gary had been reading the newspaper again. Something about Nazi hunters had caught his eye. 'Haven't they got any new news? That's ancient, that is, they're still chasing them old boys (the Nazis). Want to leave them alone. That was ages ago. They're old men now, what good would it do. Locking up old men, the pricks, pissing waste of time.'

Gary had a solution though, 'No, that's too good for them. Give them a good kicking and get them to sort out the sun-bed problem on holiday. If they die from it, sod 'em. Don't hang the pricks though, that's cruel that is.'

Eight - Pauline

The lady

In an age not long passed, Pauline would have been considered a lady. Mannered and polite, contained yet warm, charming in 'the lady of the manor' kind of way. Sherry was her drink, Harvey's luncheon dry, a dignified drink and just right for her. Clearly beautiful when younger, still beautiful now. A different kind of beauty, altered by the years, changed, but who is to say lessened. Well dressed in expensive clothes and though there seemed to be an air of arrogance about her, she was anything but. Particular about her appearance though and proud within herself.

Pauline lived now in warden controlled apartment. Pleasant, but nothing it would seem, to her previous homes. We delivered wines to her from time to time, along with her sherry. The people in these apartments would take turns to invite one another for drinks. Widows and widowers, mostly anyway; alone except for visiting relatives or friends, or each other now.

Pictures from her previous home, clearly a grand place, were hung awkwardly about the flat. In places a single huge framed canvas covering almost an entire wall. Once hung on the walls of a giant stairwell perhaps, or a magnificent drawing room. Also lamps too big, out of place here, seeming as though from a different era, from another time. Large armchairs, coffee table, bookshelves and vases too, long loved. Too precious to let go, yet overwhelming here.

The wine and the sherry would be placed on the floor beside the armchair, wrong for this place right though for Pauline, her memory beginning to fail, quite suddenly, its progress assured. Right for Pauline, these things she needed familiar things in her life and routine. She needed a routine most of all.

Nine - The Yorkshire Gentleman

His bag

If Pauline could be classed a lady then here was a male version of her. Widowed sometime ago and coincidently living in the same building as Pauline. Small cans of lager were stocked especially for him and kept in the cooler. Nobody else wanted them anymore, large was the thing now, large cans, large bottles. 25cl became 33cl and 33cl became half a litre. Often with twenty percent extra thrown in free. Big is clearly better or more popular at least.

Small cans of Heineken for him though, in for them every three days or so. He always carried with him a small slightly battered shoulder bag. In his eighties now, he would freely tell you, and he'd had that bag, that same bag for thirty years. He had bought it for their first holiday abroad, his wife and he. He would often find an obtuse way to make references to his wife. Previously it had been the bag which led onto their time spent on their Spanish holiday, the Costa Brava. Today though, his reference was the cans of Heineken.

'She would never touch this stuff you know,' he said putting the cans in the bag, 'couldn't stand beer. Helps me to sleep though so it's not so bad.'

I estimated from past conversations that his wife had been dead for twenty years or more and still he tried to involve her in his everyday dealings. Still now he 'needed' her to be included.

'Thirty years,' he said tapping the bag which safely held

his six small beers. The same bag that over the years had, no doubt, held items which he would carry for his wife. A beach towel in Spain, possibly, or an umbrella in Yorkshire.

'Still going strong,' he added, and I was unsure if he was still referring to the bag or had inadvertently moved onto speaking of himself.

'Not bad I suppose,' he said as he made his way home to open one of his two nightly cans. To make his evening less lonely, perhaps to remind him of Spain or of better times and of course to help him with his sleep.

Ten - Mary and Declan

A mother and son

Mary and Declan have long been a menace to the bars and pubs of Oxford and to the shop keepers and medics of the town too. No part of the city was spared their attentions. No establishment out of bounds. Nowhere that sold alcohol was overlooked or forgotten once visited. They would do their rounds, visiting and being refused mostly, bar after bar and store upon store. Randomly, or so it seemed but these visits were anything but random. By the time the cycle had been completed, Mary reasoned that they could be served. Or given drink or charity or pity. Mary reasoned correctly.

Often over a period of months landlords would be replaced in pubs, shops and businesses would change hands. New people, new faces behind the bars and counters now. These newcomers would not know of Mary and Declan. Sometimes in these places they would be served.

A long standing street drinker and for as long as anyone could remember, inseparable from Declan her son and like Mary he enjoyed a drink or two. Emotionally unstable and physically impaired having contracted severe frostbite many years ago, Declan was wheelchair bound. His mother was now his carer as well as the person who sourced drink for them both. And, it was wildly held in addition to these things of carer and supplier of alcohol, that Mary was her son's lover too.

Today Mary was standing in the doorway asking for two bottles of medium sherry. Declan was in his wheelchair blocking the doorway. In her time Mary had been a clever lady. Was clever still. Though that intelligence had now been transformed into a devious thing. She needed to be calculating as she needed to find new ways of obtaining the alcohol so vital to them both. And though she knew well enough that she was never served here, still on her bi-monthly rounds she would try. There had been a time when Mary would be sold her sherry. Though after an accumulation of incidents and aggression, culminating in her spreading her legs and urinating on the floor of the shop, she was no longer served. Defiant and angry that day, frustrated that her behaviour should be challenged and that her right to purchase was about to be curtailed, she had pulled her underwear to one side and still standing she had soaked the floor. A statement perhaps as well as a display of frustration and anger. If she were made to leave, forced against her will then she would leave her scent behind. That would remain and someone would need to clear up her mess.

Mary had been refused again earlier today but now she stood in the doorway, a bottle of sherry in either hand. Declan in his wheelchair on the pavement outside. Mary, wily Mary, had got someone else to purchase the sherry on her behalf. Ecstatic at this moment she danced a jig of joy. A victory dance. Swigging from one of the bottles and showing it to me. They were set for now Mary and Declan. 'I have outsmarted you,' she said as she continued her dance. And she had. I almost wanted to dance myself to join her in her moment of success. To share in the elation she was experiencing. Then she was gone pushing the wheelchair along the road. The wheelchair that held the

son, who many said was her lover too and in his lap now the bottles of sherry. One no longer full. Opened in celebration perhaps of obtaining the sherry. Possibly though on simply surviving another hard fraught day. Or for outsmarting a shop keeper.
Only they would know which, Mary and Declan. Only they would know for sure.

Eleven - The Complainers

Mrs A and the Kettle chips

Mrs A wanted to buy some Kettle chips just as we were closing for the day. Mrs A wanted a particular flavour. We stocked eight types, eight flavours of Kettle chips but sadly not the one that Mrs A wanted, in fact, had visited here specifically for. We had clearly let her down badly. She would though, she said generously, choose one all the same, even though she was disappointed with the selection on offer. 'Dismayed' was the word she had used. 'Price?' she asked, managing the tricky manoeuver of simultaneously looking down her nose at both me and the offending crisps. And though she had I am sure purchased them from us on previous occasions and must have had some idea of the price, still she was appalled.

'How much?' she said sounding like Lady Bracknell, 'How much?' she asked again though she now knew the price, 'They are ten pence cheaper in Sainsbury's,' she informed me.

Sainsbury's was five miles away, petrol would be consumed, time used and Sainsbury's had massive buying power. Also of course they would buy huge quantities of one product, even Horseradish flavoured Kettle chips. No doubt ten pence less at Sainsbury's.

Clearly we had failed her, ruined her evening if not her entire day. She picked up a packet of cheese flavoured crisps and held it as though it were infected, diseased. She paid for the foul things and left the shop distressed at the extra ten pence she had been charged for a product she had never really wanted in the first place.

Twelve - Sylvia and Peter

Choosing wine together

Peter rarely called into the shop these days. Frail now and in his eighties, less trusting of his body, acknowledging its increasing betrayal. His partial loss of hearing also added to his reluctance to leave the house. Today though he and Sylvia had walked the half a mile or so to the shops.

Sylvia would place an order with us most weeks. Cinzano Bianco, Fundador brandy, AME Herbal cordial and usually a mixed case of wine. Good wines, but not too expensive. Sylvia would always trust our recommendations regarding these. When they had consumed the wines she would return to thank us again, for their value and for their quality, often declaring them 'super' or 'splendid'. She stopped short of 'spiffing', though I expected it any time.

Sylvia sounded surprised and grateful each time we arranged a delivery as though it were a great treat or a service beyond any reasonable expectation. These days Peter would walk only with the use of a stick. Always though, either on his visits here or taking delivery of the Spanish brandy and Cinzano, he would transfer his walking stick, move it temporarily from the right hand to his left hand. Transfer it to allow him to offer a handshake to the person behind the counter that day or to welcome whoever had performed the kindness of the delivery of wines to his home.

Peter was charming. He was dignified and gracious and his

manners were impeccable. Peter was also, still very handsome. Dressed today immaculately in a well cut beige suit, blue patterned tie and crisp white shirt. His strong cultured features untouched by age. Sylvia's evident pride in her husband revealed that she was aware of his beauty, physical or otherwise. Always Sylvia involved Peter in the choosing of the wines.

'Shall we be daring and try one from Argentina?' she asked.

They had lived there once many years ago.

'That would be fun wouldn't it?' she added.

Peter agreed that it would indeed saying that they had always enjoyed the wines from that country before adding that Sylvia used to have quite a liking for their Chardonnay, as he recalled.

Sylvia always presented as a confident woman. Upper middle class, well educated, well connected and secure within herself. When she was with Peter she was still all these things, but there was something more, something else. When she was in his presence not only did she seem complete, but she was flirtatious towards him. Her face shone like a love struck teenager, her pride in the man she had bewitched evident. This handsome, intelligent, elegant man standing here beside her. Her life's love, her Peter.

Today Sylvia kept their visit brief, no doubt she did not want to tire him. It was better if they could venture out together, if only for brief periods but as often as they could. Get out of the house, to buy the bread from the bakers, cheese from the delicatessen and wine from the wine shop. Get out as often as was possible to remind people he was still here, still in the world. Still part of it and as for her, as for Sylvia, she would continue to show off her beautiful man, while she could and while he was able.

Sylvia was aware that would not be for too much longer. Peter would understand that, and no doubt as they had always shared everything, talked about everything, they would have discussed that moment too.

Thirteen - The Students

May-Day

Our busiest day of the year was not Christmas Eve or New Years Eve, neither was it the cup final, the Queen's birthday or any ones birthday or anniversary. It was the evening before the first of May. May Day. The people of Oxford and in particular its students had made this the most celebrated night of the year. The celebrations would begin early in the evening of the
30th April and up to and including lunch time of May 1st, May Day.

The store was packed with well-dressed and excited students. Stocking up for the long night ahead and covering their options regarding how quickly they wanted to get drunk and which would be their drink of choice to attain that condition. Some were buying Pimms. Many were buying Champagne, from the house Champagne to Bollinger and Tattinger and for some even Dom Perignon. Mostly price was not a necessary consideration. Virtually all though were including vodka. House vodka, Absolut, Stolichnaya, Grey Goose, vodkas flavoured with chillies or lemons. Every brand of vodka. But vodka there must be if they intended to achieve the combination of getting extremely drunk whilst managing to stay awake throughout the night.

We never had any problems with students. They were often boisterous and exuberant but never aggressive. And they would spend. Away from home for the first time and from the discipline this implied and with seemingly limitless amounts of money at their disposal.

Often purchases would be paid for on a debit or credit card issued by Coutts, or Platinum cards issued by other banks. Less prestigious perhaps but still with a limit set high regarding borrowing on the card, if a limit was set at all. The students would make for the town centre on leaving the store. Heading eventually for Maudlin Bridge but stopping at one or two pubs on the way. Some though would head for their own colleges where a ball was being held. The boys looking dapper and cool in their dinner jackets and the girls dressed in ball gowns. Not yet old enough to look elegant and beautiful, often looking instead as though they were children playing dressing up. Which in fact they were. These same students, some of them at least, would call in again in the morning for orange juice or water. Bedraggled and disheveled now. Dinner suits or gowns wet and mudded from jumping into the river from Maudlin Bridge. A custom to accompany the choir which sang from the College chapel at 5am.

The exuberance and all elegance gone now the students would take themselves home or back to their room while some would visit one of the pubs specially licensed to open early for breakfast on May day. To continue the celebrations, unwilling to allow this time to end. Acknowledging on one level or another that this was a special time in their lives. Perhaps the most special. They would line their stomachs with bacon and eggs and reflect on the night that had passed. For some a rite of passage. An unlikely step towards adulthood and responsibility. For others a show of privilege and of position and of wealth.

Fourteen - Mr Mitchell

Mr Mitchell

Mr Mitchell had been one of our earliest customers. Coming in on the first day of trading and ever present since. He would usually call in around lunchtime. A period when the store was often busy with people from the local factory or offices coming in for soft drinks and snacks for their breaks.

Often too they would take the opportunity of the lunch break to pick up something for later, intended for when they arrived home after a long day's work. A bottle of wine for dinner or a pack of beers to see them through Coronation Street or EastEnders, Match Of The Day or The Love Boat. Tonic water would be bought to accompany the gin they still had left over from the weekend. Or lemonade for the vodka, or soda for the whisky.

Mr Mitchell however, was not interested in Gin and Tonic or wine. Mr Mitchell only ever purchased Mann's brown ale. A fine beer with a long and well respected tradition. At that time many beers were sold in reusable bottles. A deposit charged on the bottle and refunded on its return. Something that worked well but has no place, unfortunately, in today's consumer society.

Mr Mitchell always took some time to take his brown ales from the shelf. If we had thought about this at all then it would simply have been put down to his age. A man in his late 70's and not in a great hurry to return to the house he lived in alone following the loss of his wife some years ago. In time though we came to realise the lingering by the shelves was nothing to do with age or an empty house but something else altogether.

Adele knew him, he had lived in the neighbourhood for many years, as she herself had. And in fact had been a customer of the store before we owned it. It was a delicatessen back then but the elderly owners had somewhat lost heart. Much of the responsibility in the venture and of the work being left to Adele who was an employee of the business even then. She knew Mr Mitchell to say good morning to in the street or at the bus stop but that, apart from his visits to us, was the extent of their interactions.

Mr Mitchell would take his purchases from the shelf and put them in his shopping bag before bringing them to the counter. A lot of people, usually older people did that. It was quite normal. He would then remove the bottles of brown ale, two bottles and place them on the counter. Then he would present the empties to have the refund on them deducted from the cost. But there were four empties. There were always four empties.

We had suspected, known really, for some time that Mr Mitchell was paying for two bottles of brown ale but taking four. His hands shook as he paid for his beers. And as he did so he was asked about the others in the bag. We were inexperienced, naïve. The drinks trade and all that went with it was new to us.

Mr Mitchell took the other beers from his bag and hands trembling more now looked in the small purse he carried for money to pay for them. There was no extra money. He was told that he could keep the beers and that there would be no charge for them. He was also told that he was fortunate that the police were not being called. But in future he would no longer be served here. Of course, it would have been impossible to let anyone come in and help themselves to whatever they wanted. No purchase necessary. No business could begin to function in that way. But I doubt it would have been so bad or so damaging for us to allow an old man the comfort of an extra beer or two to make life less empty. To alleviate boredom just a little to anaesthetise loneliness. Numbing it with a few beers and removing its dull ache, for a while at least.

It may have been my imagination or something else but I thought he looked more hunched, more frail as he left the store. And I had seen the fear and shame on his face when the police were mentioned. It hadn't been our intention to frighten or to shame him. Merely to get him to stop what he was doing.

I took the empties to the store room and put them in a crate and thought about going after him to tell him there would be no problem with him using the shop now that everything was cleared up. But I felt accosting him in the street would only add to his embarrassment.

We never saw him again and heard that he had died quite suddenly six or seven weeks after his final visit to us. I hoped that our handling of the situation, our heavy handed inexperience hadn't contributed to his death. I also hoped that he hadn't died feeling like a thief. Most probably honest all his life until circumstances and temptation conspired against him.

Fifteen - Gary

The Spanish

'That's the soddin' thing to do. Sod off on a boat, see everything. No way I'm going to Spain,' he said as though I'd asked him, 'no way, forget it,' he insisted, 'those Spanish are pricks. My mate hired a moped and was run off the road by a Spanish lorry. Left him hanging on a branch. He had a few scratches on the bike. The old boy wanted eighty pounds to sort it out; eighty pounds for a scratch. My mate gave him twenty and told him to piss off.'

Gary had tears of laughter in his eyes at the thought of this. 'Then my mate,' he continued, composing himself, 'saw the old boy's van outside and nicked the keys when he wasn't looking and lobbed them into the pissin' sea. He sat in the bar next door and roared as the old boy searched everywhere for his keys. The prick, that'll teach him to rip off the English'.

Sixteen - John Thaw

The actor

It was not unusual for celebrities to call into the shop. This part of town was home to actors, playwrights, television journalists and presenters, writers, poets and painters. Also Oxford with its colleges and its history was a popular place for making films or television programmes.

It shouldn't have been too much of a surprise to see John Thaw enter the shop and approach the counter, even though I knew they were filming locally, still though I was surprised.

'A bottle of Smirnoff and a bottle of Bells please,' he said. His delivery neither hostile or overtly pleasant. I was a big fan of the actor and had followed his career from the Sweeney to Morse. Watched him too, playing minor roles in some big films and had thoroughly enjoyed his performance, untraceable accent and all in, '*Goodnight Mr Tom*'. In this he played an elderly widower who befriends and finally adopts a boy orphaned during the war. The programme was unashamedly sentimental and something of a tearjerker and John Thaw is excellent in it, as he is in most things.

It was Morse though that had brought him here today. An episode was being filmed around the corner. A house was to have its doors and windows blown out in a simulated explosion and scenes were apparently to be shot on the canal tow path and one of the local pubs. It was the talk of the area and quite exciting too.

I wrapped the two bottles of spirits for the actor and placed them in a carrier bag. We had a kind of unspoken policy in the store that we should not react or refer to a person's fame or the profession that had gained them their fame. I was attempting to do the same thing now.

Years later I read his wife Sheila Hancock's biography of her husband. She openly says many times that he was prone to depression and a heavy drinker, though she made clear that he was often not a happy drinker.

I told him the amount due for the whisky and the vodka. He paid me neither speaking or smiling. Though he did not manifest any semblance of rudeness or arrogance. He simply wanted to pay for and obtain his drinks. I thanked him and he nodded slightly in return and left the shop to return to the house that was to have its windows and doors blown out for an episode of Inspector Morse. To immerse himself in his work and become someone else for the day.

Seventeen – Adele

Adele and the Spitfire

Adele had never been late for work. It wasn't in her character to be late or in the collective consciousness of her generation. Today Adele was late. Thirty minutes passed before I phoned her, concerned that something serious, possibly life threatening had happened.

'I'm quite all right my dear,' she said sounding positively cordial. Her voice taking on the pseudo posh tone that she sometimes would adopt when in the company of someone she regarded as her social superior, 'I have a visitor,' she added, 'But I shan't be long as I believe he is about to leave now.'

Adele arrived in a taxi some twenty minutes after our conversation. Her eyes were bright and her cheeks were rosy. Adele looked elated. 'I'm so sorry,' she said putting on the apron she always wore during working hours, 'You see,' she began, her tone being the epitome of normality, 'A squadron of RAF Spitfire aeroplanes were forced to land in our close. The Squadron Leader, a handsome young man, accepted my offer of a cup of tea and a biscuit while his men repaired and refueled the aircraft.'

Adele had wasted no time getting to work and was now busy cleaning the brass on the beer pumps and tidying the counter.

'Such a lovely polite young man and quite dashing,' she said her voice completely normal save for the clipped vowels she was still using. She continued to relate all that the squadron leader had told her regarding their 'sortie' to France and that they had lost one aircraft and its pilot. 'A good man and a fine pilot by all accounts.' Adele carried on working as normal throughout the shift adding nothing further about the incident. In fact she only spoke of it this one time. I have no idea if she ever 'saw' her dashing young RAF man again. Landing his Spitfire in her close and calling on her for a cup of tea and a biscuit while his plane was being repaired and refueled.

Eighteen - Alex

The drunk and his rags

Alex is an erratic, unpredictable drunk, one day outgoing, upbeat and border line charming, the next an angry cauldron of alcohol and regret, fury and despair. We would serve the charmer but could not serve the angry ranting Alex, abusive to staff and customers alike, aggressive and sly by turns.

Today, on being refused, his foul language polluting the atmosphere, he became instantly threatening.

'I know there's a baby up there,' he said pointing to the accommodation above the shop, 'I know a baby lives there. I'll put petrol through the door and burning rags when every ones asleep. Petrol,' he said again and more quietly now with an angry, crafty expression on his face and a smile of someone who would get his way, no matter by which means. A smile intended to imply that he would not be denied, a victors smile.

'Petrol through the letter box,' he said again, the sly, crafty expression fixed on his face. A comic book villain or something from a Charles Dickens novel. Real though this villain. Such an easy thing to do, burning rags and fuel through a letter box. The simplicity making it all the more frightening. Such a thing to threaten, and who knows, possibly such an act as well. To suggest the taking of lives over something as seemingly mundane as a few beers. To threaten the life of a child, for a can of lager.

Nineteen - Pauline

The best of the lady

Pauline had an economy with words. Warm without smiling, likeable with little effort and no apparent intention of being so. And I liked Pauline, I liked her almost immediately with her good manners and her pleasant directness.

She was aware that we were happy to deliver and that being the case, 'Would it possible to send a few things to her apartment?' she asked.

The way that she said it, though simply asking for a small thing that was a usual part of our service made it feel as though it would be a privilege. Like being chosen by the head boy to play for the football team or asked to make a speech at a friend's wedding.

Pauline ordered a mixed case of wine, some red, some white within an expressed price range.

'You choose please,' she said. She told me the address, Wyndham House and added two bottles of Harvey's Luncheon Dry Sherry to the order.

Wyndham House was an up-market apartment building for the elderly and for the wealthy. A safe and pleasant environment in which to undertake your final years.

We agreed a time for the wines to be delivered and then the transaction completed she thanked me and told me it was 'most kind' and left. To go back to Wyndham House or to do a little more shopping. Simple enough things which were easy enough to carry out for now at least. This was to be the best of her, the best of Pauline. In a surprisingly short space of time her clarity would begin to fail. Until the day she would stand in the doorway and ask 'Do you know me?'

Not the more usual but still awkward 'Do I know you?' that most of us have asked at times or felt the need to ask. Knowing someone's face but failing to recall how you knew them and reluctant to say so. Meeting the dentist in the street, or the butcher in the queue for the cinema. Familiar faces but difficult to place when taken out of context. Pauline's situation would not be so easily resolved.

I barely knew her at all at this point but by the time she asked her question, 'Do you know me?' I would know her fairly well, all of us here would. It would be Pauline herself who would strive for an answer then. But thankfully not now. That day though would come, was already set in place. It would not be so long before it arrived.

Twenty - The Yorkshire Gentleman

His wife and good weather

As always when he came in for his beers, he had his trusty bag hanging from his shoulder. The transaction was to be swift today what with the weather being 'so good', he wanted to 'do a few things'.

He placed his six small beers in the bag and thanked me, now ready to go about his business.

'She would have loved this you know,' he said, indicating the weather, 'bit warm for me but not for my wife. The warmer the better for her. Couldn't get it too warm. Oh well,' he added.

The smile that had temporarily brightened his face passing now. Then he was gone. Left the shop to do his few things on this hot summer's day which his wife, dead for twenty years, would have loved.

Twenty One - Charlie

Charlie likes everything these days

It was Charlie who brought our Tuesday delivery this week. The usual mixture of beers and wines and a few seasonal drinks. This being summer a dozen cases of Pimms No 1 were also with the delivery.

Though the orders would change with the seasons, these days Charlie never would. 'Tally ho,' or, 'Chin chin,' he would say passing the cases of Pimms from his truck, implying something to do with its upper class associations. 'Tastes good at the races,' he said as he moved the boxes, 'Ascot does a lovely one, plenty of fruit and a sprig of mint. You don't usually get mint,' he added, 'but I like it with mint. It helps lift the ingredients, sharpens them up.' Charlie likes his Pimms at the race track.

Charlie tended to like most things these days. Since getting out of the pub trade, simple things had gained new meaning for him. Or perhaps they had only been rediscovered; lost for a time simple pleasures. A summer drink, music, non-aggressive communication in the work place, lost to him for a while. Life's small joys, hidden, buried amid the pressures of managing a town centre pub and the responsibility that comes with that.

'That's about it for today,' said Charlie handing down the last case of Pimms, 'Toodle pip old chap,' he said as he got into his cab keeping up his Pimms theme, 'Tally ho,' he added smiling as he drove away.

Twenty Two - The Priest

The priest and his Tuscan wines

It's no new thing that a priest should enjoy a drink. No revealing of a great unspoken truth. Italian wines were this priest's preference in particular the red wines of Tuscany; good but not too expensive. Chianti Classico he liked and Montepulchiano D'bruszzo. Brunello di Montalchino he had encountered in the Italian village itself. And though he could appreciate it was a fine wine indeed still it was not entirely to his liking. Its powerful body and strong intense taste were for him a little overbearing.

'Heavy on the palate,' he said before patting his trousers, 'and heavy on the pocket.'

He had travelled extensively in Italy but most of his time there had been spent in Tuscany. It was here that he liked the most and here that he felt most at home. He had developed a taste for the wines of the area and an understanding of its people. To him the Italians had become like their wines, sometimes complex, occasionally bitter, but usually ripe, wholesome and full of sun. Perhaps some of this had rubbed off on the priest during his many visits. For certainly he was a man himself full of sunlight and full also of the enjoyment of life. Tuscany may have helped with this but I suspect it was in his nature, as it was his nature that had made him become a priest. To help people, to make people happy as he was happy. Help his parishioners to relish all that there is in this world before moving onto the next.

He smiled often and always had a short anecdote to tell during our transactions. Surprisingly, to me, he would tell jokes that were a little bawdy and on occasion leaning towards racist in content. I did not believe that there was anything bigoted about him, bawdy yes. Maybe the wine satisfied one appetite and innuendo of a sexual or racial nature helped to address another. Bringing something out of the shade to bathe it in light plainer for all to see. Most likely it seemed to me the jokes and the stories were his way of saying that he may be a priest, a man of the cloth. Still though he was like us, of the people, just like you and just like me.

A small coincidence had occurred a few months back. The priest had been officiating at my godson's baptism. I did not let on that I knew him when our eyes briefly met. I wasn't sure of the protocol regarding a merchant, a seller of wines in a place of worship. Anyway he was busy with Jack, baptising the ten month old child. Nobody could know that he would be called upon again in a matter of weeks to perform a less joyous service for this tiny boy. Jack died in his sleep a victim of sudden infant death syndrome. There can be few things more devastating for a parent or so cruel to a child so young as to be beyond innocence.

The priest himself had told me on this visit to the shop that he was to undergo a routine operation, the removal of gallstones or kidney stones I don't quite remember which. 'In and out in a day and a half,' he said before cracking another dubious joke.

Something about Stevie Wonder not knowing he was black and though he was blind, things could be worse.

'See you Thursday,' he said cheerily as he left the shop with his carrier bag containing two bottles of Sangiavese and some crisps and chocolate.

He did not come in on Thursday or Friday or Saturday either. A week later his son called in. His son was never as warm or jovial as his father. He would come in though, once a month or so on his visits up from London. He would always stop to buy some wine for his father before calling on him. Normally he would say only a brief hello before choosing the wines from the shelves. This time though he simply stood at the counter. He looked older than he had on his previous visits and his skin seemed grey and his eyes were swollen and red.

Later I thought the greyness of his skin was probably due to the physical and emotional strain he had been under. Attempting to compose himself over a period of time, time that seemed both fleeting and endless.

'I thought I should let you know,' he said finally ,'my father went in for an operation a week ago.'

I nodded my understanding of this.

'He never regained consciousness. I thought I should let you know. He always enjoyed coming in here, he would often say how warmly he was greeted on his visits. His heart gave out under the anaesthetic, I just thought you should know,' he said again.

I told him how sorry I was and for what it was worth we all thought the world of his father.

'He knew,' he said, a pale smile attempting to establish itself in an effort to ward off tears.

'Thank you all though,' he said before leaving the shop. No blood red Chianti purchased today, no Sangiavese either.

Twenty Three - The Complainers

Mrs B and her nuts

Mrs B wanted to buy some nuts as she was expecting visitors. Was it cheaper, she wondered, to buy three small packets or one of the larger size, which was better? She wanted to know if it was cheaper to purchase one type of nut.

With the small bags she could offer her guests a selection, cashews perhaps and peanuts, possibly pistachios. Mrs B just didn't know. Were cashews better than pistachios? The peanuts were far cheaper, although the macadamia nuts were, she said 'outrageous'. In addition, her guests would no doubt expect a drink of some kind with their snacks. Would a can of lager be enough for two? The nuts though were still troubling her. She was concerned about the varying salt content; she didn't like too much salt. Perhaps her guests were quite the opposite. If it were up to her, which in fact it was, she would give them a glass of dry sherry, but these days people preferred lager 'didn't they?' Mrs B picked up a can of Castlemaine 4X, it had been pointed out to her that this was not a strong lager. A point clearly in its favour as she didn't want her guests to be leaving inebriated. The Castlemaine was eventually joined on the counter by a small packet of KP peanuts and two small packets of cashew nuts. One last thing though before she paid, Did we have the beer cold, as this one was warm. They may call at any time and she should hate to offer them warm beer or seemingly peanuts that were too salty, Macadamia nuts that were 'outrageous' or lager of above a certain strength.

Twenty Four - Dennis

The brewery rep

Dennis always brought something for us when he visited on behalf of the company he represented. Sometimes it would be pint glasses with the logo of the brewery's flagship ale embossed upon them, or bar towels with 'Wadworth 6X' emblazoned across them.

At Christmas time there would be calendars. Each month featuring one of their pubs, usually interior shots and always in timeless black and white. The photographs would show shiny faced men holding frothing pints of ale congregated around the bar area talking and laughing warmly. The women too would be enjoying themselves and of course enjoying the ale. Though for them the beer would be served in half pint glasses still featuring the company logo. Each page of the calendar would be a variation on a theme. In winter months roaring log fires would feature strongly keeping the drinkers warm happy and contented. The fire would suggest that there was no better place to be on a cold winter's day. And while the smiling ruddy faces of the customers would support that, it was really the pint pots of 6X or Old Timer that confirmed it. Who wouldn't want to be somewhere like that with the warmest fires and the finest company?

Little on the calendars was changed for the summer months though the fires would be gone. A display of dry flowers taking their place until the weather turned again. The doors and windows would be open to allow the warm summer air to enter and to show the sunlight contrasting with the more subdued light of the pubs interior. The same men and women were here though possibly not the same but similar enough to make no difference. And beer was flowing and people still smiling. The landlord was ever jovial and the lives of all seemed rich and full partly due to their choice of drinking establishment but due mainly to the wisdom they had shown in their choice of beer.

'For you,' Dennis said, filling the counter with beer mats and notepads bar trays, beer glasses and an ice bucket. Dennis always smiled or cracked a joke on his visits, today there was no sign of either.

The trays and the glasses and the mats were useful to us. People seemed to enjoy merchandise. An ice bucket given away with a large order of wine, free glasses with a case of beer, and bar towels and beer mats were always well received.

Dennis looked as if he wanted to speak but somehow the words would not come. Instead he took a deep breath, shook his head and sighed. I poured him a pint of ale and as I passed it to him I asked him what was wrong. We always offered Dennis a beer on his visits to us. I think most of pubs he called upon did the same. He always accepted it. It may have been his polite way of checking that his company's beer was being well kept, the pipes clean and the ale fresh. Or maybe he simply enjoyed a beer or two as he went about his daily business. Still it had become something of a tradition and though I only joined him with a coke, it created a short period of time shared. He was not a sales rep' and I was not a customer. He had no interest is selling me something that I did not need. And I had no intention of nailing him down further on

Stuart Wilson

discounts. During these moments over a shared drink it was closer to two old friends talking in a pub than any kind of business transaction.

'They're retiring me,' he said, finally making the words come, 'and this will be my last visit.'

Dennis had been with the same company all of his working life, ever since the age of fifteen.

He had told me during one of our bar chats that it was all he had ever known and that he neither wanted to or would be capable of doing anything else. Dennis took a sip of his beer and fidgeted with the stacks of beer mats as he did so. He was close to tears though clearly attempting to keep his emotions under control.

'They have to,' he said, 'I 'm sixty-five now and it's their policy so they have no choice,' he added, his loyalty to the company he had served for fifty years still evident. 'Not their fault really. I asked them if I could go cash in hand or part time. They could cut my hourly rate, anything really but no they said it wasn't possible.'

For Dennis it wasn't about the money, perhaps it signified to him that his usefulness had passed and therefore much of his reason for living had diminished also. Had it forced him to consider his own mortality or was he simply concerned about getting under his wife's feet having spent so much of his life outside of the house. Worried that she may get bored with him, fed up with seeing him moping about the place, interrupting her routine and getting in the way. He had never felt he had ever been in the way in his working life.

I suggested that he would be welcome to call at these places knowing it was not the right thing to say but unsure of what to put in its place. Dennis took another sip of his beer and seemed disappointed with my suggestion.

'For what?' he asked, 'what would be the point?'

Dennis shook my hand and thanked me for our custom throughout the years. I thanked him in return telling him it had been our pleasure and to please call in when he had the chance.

Dennis finished his beer and said goodbye, 'Anyway,' he added on his way to the door, 'you've got another rep now, a younger one.'

And as he said it after fifty years of conducting himself correctly and behaving in a certain way he somehow managed to smile.

Twenty Five - The Drunks

Drunk X

Drunk X came in every-day for two months. He would invariably be the first customer of the day. Punctual and organized, and though always under the influence of the previous day's session, still he was never any trouble and always polite.

In his time, which had passed now, you could tell he had been handsome. His eyes were still good though, deep and brown and in spite of the hardship of his existence, kindly. His hair was thick and curly and he looked like an Irish tinker. But in fact he came from the midlands of England, Birmingham maybe or Coventry. Sherry was his drink, English sherry as it was the most inexpensive, and medium because 'it wasn't too sweet or too dry.'

On occasion he would have a friend with him, huge and silent and brooding. Perhaps though he was not brooding, maybe there was simply nothing he wished to say. He was dressed, his friend, the same whatever the weather.

Dressed in a blanket with a hole cut out to allow it to fit snugly over his head. The blanket at one time, you could tell, had been bright yellow; now though it was filthy and matted. He always carried with him a black bin liner which held all of his belongings. Sometimes they would arrive in a taxi timed perfectly to coincide with the shop opening its doors for the day's trading.

They would buy their sherry, and then spend the day with other drinkers, by the bridge over the canal.

Drunk X began musing aloud today, 'I had a good woman once,' he said, 'the best. I didn't look after her and I went with other women. They had nothing on her. She found out though more than once and threw me out. The best,' he said again.

'She was right to do it. I should have looked after her, I should have.'

His friend was leaving the shop now with his sherry. He'd probably heard this story many times and was keen to get to the bridge, to sit beside the canal and begin the day's drinking.

'If you've got a good woman,' said drunk X before following his friend, 'you should look after her you should cherish her.'

Twenty Six - Gary

The solicitor

'Sodding briefs,' Gary said by way of today's greeting, following up with, 'can't tell which side they're on.' Gary was referring to his solicitor, 'Wants to settle for fifty grand.'

He paused for a moment allowing a gap I think for my response. I wasn't sure what response would be appropriate so said nothing.

'Fifty sodding grand,' he said a little louder this time concerned that he may not have made himself understood the first time, 'for making me a cripple,' he added for clarification and for effect, 'is that all I am worth to them? It's an insult not an offer.'

Gary disliked being insulted. As he spoke he went about the shop gathering his usual drinks and snacks or a variation on them just to keep things interesting. Hula Hoops instead of crisps, a topic to replace a Mars bar and so on. And considering his perceived disability he moved quite freely as he did so. Gary liked variation, what he didn't like, or one of the things he didn't like was solicitors. 'Wankers,' he said taking a cold bottle of coke from the chiller and putting it on the counter. Gary had always said he wanted one hundred thousand pounds for his industrial accident a figure that his solicitor had himself arrived at after taking all relevant factors into account. The lack of a protective barrier that would have prevented his forklift ending up in the canal with him trapped beneath it. In addition the absence of a nurse or medically trained person on site and the fact that he was moved before the ambulance crew arrived, possibly making things worse by doing this. And of course the debilitating effect of the injuries and the constant pain it caused him. The terrible searing pain that according to Gary was always with him but at times was so bad he was barely able to endure it. At times he had said so excruciating that he would be reduced to tears.

'I am worth more than that surely?' he said, and feeling that he genuinely required an answer or reassurance, I told him that he was certainly, and asked him what he planned to do. I was sure that he would have a plan, Gary always had a plan.

'Screw' em,' he replied, his tactics clear, 'I am not having it. I told him that,' he said referring to his solicitor, 'It was his idea,' he said, meaning the original compensation figure rather than the accident in the canal, 'and now he reckons the company is running out of money. Not doing so well or something.'

Gary threw his lunch into a carrier bag, annoyed at the offer that he considered an insult and angry at the solicitor who was prepared to betray him, ready to sell him out for half of what he was worth.

'Running out of money,' he said picking up his bag ready to make his way back to the workplace that had, through their negligence almost put him in a wheelchair.

'Should have thought of that before they went about buggering up peoples' backs. Tight sods,' he added extending the scope of his opinion and rubbing his injured back as he left the store.

Twenty Seven - Mr S

The Sanatogen Man

Some drinks, like fashions, or hairstyles attain a certain amount of popularity and then for no obvious reason they are gone. Tab Cola, Watneys Red Barrel, Babycham, Snowballs, even certain whisky's or vodka's make an impact and for no obvious reason go suddenly out of favour. Sometimes, as is the case with vodkas or beers, they will be replaced by something more exotic. Vodkas from the Ukraine, or from Poland or Russia flavoured with chillies or limes. Beers blended with fruits, raspberries, apricots, cherries. Ales mixed with chocolate or beers that do not smell or taste of beer tasting instead like lemonade or cranberry juice.

The name of a simple bitter will after centuries of being known by the brewery's name suddenly need a makeover. Bitter or best, brown or mild will no longer suffice. Sometimes Hogsback, Hobgoblin or Dogs Bollocks is considered a better option for the sake of image and therefore the sake of sales.

Sanatogen tonic wine is one such product. 'Sanatogen Tonic Wine'. Difficult now to find in shops and rarely stocked by suppliers. We had one customer though who would call in every week for two bottles of 'his tonic wine'. And though on these visits to us he seldom had anything of great interest to say, still he was always cheerful, smiling and warm. A picture of contentment and someone though clearly advanced in years still enjoyed life and the simple things that life had to offer. He made no secret of the fact that he regarded a nightly tipple of Sanatogen to be one of these things. In fact more than that, this evening ritual could even be considered to be one of life's great joys.

'Two bottles please,' he said, neither bothering or needing to name the product.

His order could have been wrapped, payment accepted and bagged without the need for a word to be spoken.

'Of course,' I replied playing my part in this ritual, 'and how are you today?'

Sanatogen Tonic Wine, no longer available in chemists as it had once had been due to its medicinal content. We ordered it in especially for him and though a few bottles were stocked on the shelves - placed beside Dubbonet and the Cinzano Bianco - he was the only person whoever purchased it.

Mr S. as we called him was grateful too.

'Can't get this anywhere else now,' he would tell us on each of his visits, followed by the revelation that, 'we have a glass of this, my wife and I, and a sandwich every evening before going to bed. It's lovely and we sleep so well.'

Although the repetitive nature of this comment could in the wrong hands, have become incredibly boring, from him it was anything but. He said it with such vitality, such childlike enthusiasm that it was difficult not to be taken into his world, for a moment at least. It was clearly so much more than a drink, a glass of wine. It was a way of life. A provider on a daily basis of a shared and special moment for him and his wife. An allotted period put aside just for them no matter what else the day would bring. It was also a precursor to a sound and satisfying sleep.

He looked healthy, contented and well. Maybe that was his disposition or perhaps it was something else. The sandwich and the wine and the special moment set aside to be shared with his wife.

The label on the bottle announced that it was an 'uplifting and beneficial tonic wine'. A bold boast certainly but one that Mr S and his wife would seem to confirm.

Twenty Eight - The Complainers

Mrs D and her special port

Mrs D was 'nonplussed' today. You could have guessed it from her demeanour though she had been good enough to inform us herself regarding this.

'Nonplussed,' she said, and seemingly more than a little annoyed. The reason for her annoyance was due almost entirely to the fact that we had run out of 'her port'.

Mrs D would buy a bottle of Dows Special Reserve Port perhaps three times during a year, and as far as I can recall we had never been out of it before.

'Such an inconvenience,' she continued.

It had been explained to her that it was not a product that we stocked in great numbers. In fact one of the colleges had purchased our entire supply the previous day their usual stockist having sold out. Mrs D pointed out, to ensure there was to be no further misunderstanding, that this was hardly any fault of hers. Which was in fact true.

'Why didn't you simply reserve a bottle for me?' she asked, surprise and disappointment now evident in her voice.

Mrs D was shown a number of ports of similar style, quality and price but none of them had the name Dows printed on the label.

'Hardly,' she said of one, 'certainly not,' she said of others. She left the most disdain for the Cockburn's, 'I don't think so,' she said, pausing for a second before adding, 'do you?'

She was told that in addition to the suggestions regarding

an alternative that a delivery which included 'her port' would arrive on Thursday. Two days from now.

'That is no good to me,' she said, and of course it was no good to her.

Mrs D needed it now and the port I suspected, like most things in her life, should be available the instant she required them.

'I shall have to go elsewhere,' she said as though elsewhere was another country and she left a little more than nonplussed now. Surprised and disappointed and annoyed, and it was clear as she did so that she felt we had badly inconvenienced her, treated her poorly and perhaps worse of all we had shamefully let her down.

Twenty Nine - Colin Dexter

Morse's dad

A few days after John Thaw's visit, Colin Dexter called in. The filming of Inspector Morse was continuing around the corner and I assumed the writer was visiting the set to check on the progress of the episode or to engage with the actors regarding their interpretation of his characters, and the words he had written for them. Writers can be notoriously protective of their creations, seeing them in a certain way. Knowing them for longer than anyone else. Living with them sometimes for years and therefore understanding and relating to them better than anyone else.

The actor's job, it was though, to bring three dimensional life to the characters, lifting them from the page, giving them life and transporting them into people's homes. Still though it was the writer that had undergone the inception, the gestation and finally the birth. And as such, sometimes these creations would be viewed more as children than products of the imagination.

I had no way of knowing if Colin Dexter would view Inspector Morse in that way but seeing him good naturedly pottering about the wines somehow I felt it was possible.

'Can you recommend a couple of bottles?' he asked, 'one red, one white, nothing too fancy.'

He smiled warmly as he spoke and his eyes danced and twinkled mischievously giving him the look of someone who expected to be found out at any moment for something naughty they had done and had got away with for far too long.

We had recently begun stocking Mcguigans Australian wines. Top quality wines and not too expensive. These were the first wines I suggested though I intended to offer alternatives.

'Just right,' he said, 'I'll take one of each.'

In his book and now on TV Colin Dexter portrayed Oxford in a way that few people living here would recognise. A truly beautiful city, though a hotbed of murder and intrigue. Dead church wardens and murdered university dons found poisoned or with a knife in the chest. Often, gruesome killings that Morse must solve whilst sometimes falling into romance. Emotionally contained regarding his work, though desperate for love and to be loved in return.

'Thank you for your recommendations,' he said as he paid me.

It struck me how different Colin Dexter was from his creation and from the man who portrayed him. He was full of smiles and nods and eye contact. Seriously enjoying his life and comfortable with the new found fame that had come his way. The wine he had purchased for dinner with friends would be enjoyed. There would be conversation and no doubt laughter.

I thanked him and he did the same in return and left the shop to visit, I imagined, the house with the blown out windows that for now doubled as a film set. To speak with the people at work there and with the actor whose responsibility it was to make us believe in his character. And more than that, more importantly than that, to empathise, to make us care.

Thirty - Mary and Declan

Second circuit

We were long overdue a visit from Mary and her son Declan. Always a part of her cycle which took in the entire town and most of the off-licences and the shops in and around the city itself. A cycle which took somewhere in the region of six to eight weeks to complete. And then they would begin again trying their luck in every supermarket, shop or wine store. Attempting to be served sherry or cider whether or not they had previously been refused. This morning was to be our turn.

Mary was an intelligent woman and widely believed to be from a good family. Hard-working, professional people. People that perhaps enjoyed a gin and tonic after a day's work, or a glass or two of wine with the evening meal. Mary showed no such restraint. She and Declan would drink from the moment they awoke in the morning and swigging from a bottle would be the last act of every day. No teeth to be cleaned or the grime of the city wiped from their faces except for the time they spent with social services which was infrequent and generally appeared to be ineffective.

She was outside now preparing to come in, parking Declan in his wheelchair on the pavement close to the shop door. Many drunks, many alcoholics are unhappy, troubled souls. Mary didn't appear to be either. She talked incessantly and laughed often, a loud hoarse, grating laugh. Her voice thickened by alcohol and cigarettes. And even when she was abusing people, which was a regular occurrence, still she seemed to be happy. She had her boy with her at all times, a son she clearly loved, doted on would not be over estimating her position. And she was responsible for no one, only him. She had freedom and independence and the opportunity to drink sherry and cider every day, as much as she liked and for as long as she could. For Mary this situation was of her making. She had made a lifestyle choice. Something that many of us are unable, or perhaps brave enough to do.

She was stopping people as they passed, no doubt asking them to purchase sherry on her behalf knowing she would not be served. Sometimes people would cross the road before reaching them or try to ignore her as they passed. It was impossible to ignore Mary. To attempt to do so would inevitably result in a torrent of abuse and animated hand and arm movements. For us it was better if Mary was prevented from entering the shop. Once inside she would prove difficult to remove, almost impossible in fact without the usual shouting, screaming and swearing and on one occasion even urinating on the floor 'to teach us a lesson.'

She had once been a staff nurse in Dublin, an important responsible job. It was almost impossible to reconcile that Mary with the Mary now standing in the door way.

'Sherry,' she said trying to push her way into the shop. 'Medium,' ensuring that the sherry she was sold would be correct and to her taste. She was told that she would not be served and a brief explanation was given. With Mary it was an impossible situation. If you didn't explain she would assume she was being refused for no reason whatsoever. A long explanation would indicate to her that the situation was open to debate. A short explanation at times would be successful and at other times would simply serve to infuriate and ignite her. Believing that she was being dealt with curtly or disrespectfully. Today Mary ignited. Trying to force her way in aiming a kick or two as she did so. A flood of abuse erupting from her in her strong Dublin accent, some of which I had never heard before even from her. In time, though not calm, she stopped and returned to Declan in his wheelchair ready I hoped to move on.

Declan never spoke, at least I never heard a word from him and I had always assumed he was unable to walk. But now he stood and took a few steps towards the shop door. He did not seem angry or confrontational, he just looked at me with a long flat gaze, lacking expression. Neither puzzled, pleased or annoyed. Then he returned to his wheelchair and they moved away, along the road, Mary shouting but at least moving away.

Someone else's problem now Mary and her son Declan, able to walk after all. Perhaps his choice, in part at least to make him dependant on his mother as she had decided that he would be her only responsibility. And as odd as this may seem, for them, and maybe only for them, it seemed to work.

Thirty One - The Drunks

Challenged by Adele

The older street drinkers were seldom too much of a problem. They seemed to understand that there was a certain code to be observed regarding their behaviour. Even in lives that were often awash with chaos, rules, though often unspoken, needed to be adhered to just the same.

Drunk A was one such elderly drinker. In past times he would have been referred to as a tramp. He carried with him at all times a battered holdall. One handle of the bag broken, he held it in front of him with both hands, cradled as you would cradle a small dog or a child. Protected by the bag and protective too, for in it was all he owned. He usually managed to appear fairly clean although his hair was long and he wore a beard. Sometimes when his drinking sessions had been particularly prolonged or severe he was not so clean and he would occasionally soil himself as was the case today. Also he was drunk today so we could not serve him though he was not aggressive or abusive. He was simply extremely drunk and there was a pattern with drunk A and others like him. Myself or another member of staff would simply stand quietly, mindful not to make too much eye contact. And we would leave it to Adele to refuse him service.

Drunk A would complain and shout if I refused him service, no matter how politely it was put to him. But from Adele, an elderly lady, well dressed, well spoken and firm, he would accept it.

'Fair play misses,' he said when Adele informed him that he would not be getting served today as he was far too inebriated.

An old school drinker aware of the rules of the game and the restrictions that his lifestyle often would force upon him and the boundaries that lifestyle created. He may be a drinker, a drunk even, but still certain standards needed to be maintained. There remained some things that he would not do, and abusing an old lady in the pursuit of alcohol was one of them.

'Fair play,' he said again before quietly leaving the store.

Thirty Two - Sylvia and Peter

The lost girl

The little girl didn't speak on entering the shop. Probably she had been warned of the dangers of talking to strangers. She simply walked in and stood silently in front of the counter.

I smiled at her in what I hoped was a non-threatening way and waited for her parents to join her. Perhaps to buy some crisps or lemonade, or something for a snack or a drink by the river. Adele smiled too, ruby-red lipstick smudged on her teeth and spread a little beyond the designated boundaries of her lips. The child would have noticed this too. But still she registered no emotion neither did she speak a word. And there was no sign yet of her parents. Some minutes passed and the girl just waited quietly. I checked outside and could see no one, except for Sylvia making her way along the street and interacting briefly with people she knew as she did so. No mother or father were to be seen. The girl was lost.

Finally speaking now she told us she had been in town with her mummy and daddy and that she couldn't see them at all. The town centre is over a mile from the shop. With what we felt were reassuring words we told the little girl that we would telephone for her parents to come and collect her. But before doing this I gave her a seat at the counter and some crisps, a coke and some chocolate. She looked completely relaxed and untroubled and began tucking into her impromptu treats.

Sylvia came in as I spoke to the police. The girl's parents

had contacted them regarding their daughter's disappearance and I was told a police unit would be here within minutes. Sylvia, herself a parent was speaking gently to the girl, whose name was Sophie, as I finished the call.

I told Sophie that everything was fine and that her parents were on the way which seemed to increase her urgency to finish the crisps and chocolates before they arrived. We tried not to fuss over her as we waited trying instead to appear calm and confident that her mummy and daddy would arrive, which they did after a short period.

Too relived to be angry with their daughter they simply held her and kissed her. The policewoman asked a few straight forward questions, thanked us for the call and then they were gone. Not a word had been spoken from either parent to myself, Sylvia or Adele. An empty crisp packet, chocolate wrapper and coke can, at the end of the counter the only evidence that we had not imagined the entire thing.

As Sylvia purchased the wines and the Cinzano which she had originally called in for, we spoke. We talked about the girl and of the relief of her parents and one or two other things connected to the central theme of a lost child. I had never really spoken to Sylvia before. Though I knew she was well known in the area and on good terms with Magistrates, Doctors and the like. I had also heard that she adored her husband of many years and that they were as close as two people could be. I had met her husband, Peter, a man of beautiful manners and charming ways. I could see, in part at least why he was so adored by his wife. Our conversation over, Sylvia smiled warmly, and pointed to the empty wrappers on the counter as she made to leave the shop.

'Bravo,' she said, 'could have been tricky,' she added, before making her way home to discuss with Peter over a glass of chilled wine the incident of the lost girl in the wine store and the happy ending that ensued.

Thirty Three - The Students

The fight

The shop door was always kept open from spring to autumn. It was nice to get the warm breeze drifting in along with the sounds from the street; cars and bicycles and peoples' voices moving on the wind. And laughter sometimes, especially in summertime, laughter could be heard.

It was term time in September and the shop was busy with students. We were working hard to keep pace with their requirements. Pimms was selling fast along with lemonade and bags of ice. Vodka too and ice cold beer, cans of Stella Artois or bottles of lager. Becks was always popular but other 'boutique beers' would come and go. St. Paoli Girl from Germany, Sol or Corona from Mexico. Brahma beer from Brazil fading now in their popularity soon to be overtaken by the next trend. Perhaps coming from China or Thailand, or the microbreweries of Americas West Coast.

England had just played Germany in a football match, had beaten them five - one and the country was in the mood to celebrate, no doubt in a variety of ways which is usual here. But in the main the mood in the store was good. Buoyant and noisy and full of animated people. Mostly students on a regular Saturday night.

Outside in the street there was a commotion and voices could be heard, raised above the rest of the noise. Standing out because of the angry tone of the voices.

We never had any problem with the students, often loud and boisterous and on occasion arrogant, but never aggressive or abusive. Childlike in the main and like children they had no desire to hurt or injure anyone, they would much rather simply have fun.

As we served, keeping pace with the orders, my ear became attuned to the noise outside. The angry voices were becoming more raised and I could see that two young men, students I assumed, were arguing with a local man who was bespectacled and middle aged. I had no idea what the dispute was about. I carried on with the Pimms and the Smirnoff and hoped whatever it was it would soon be resolved in a civilised manner though I could still hear their voices above the rest. These students sounded to me as though they were from another era even for Oxford. Their voices as they shouted at the local man sounded like Bertie Wooster or Noel Coward.

'You would be for it if not for your glasses,' I heard one of them say, although the logic of it somehow escaped me. The middle aged man quickly removed his glasses placing them in his shirt pocket and at the same time punched Bertie Wooster or Noel Coward.

'I'm not wearing them now am I?' and it was true, the glasses were nowhere to be seen.

'My god,' said the student, holding his hand to his face, 'he's socked me in the eye,' which though of course an act of violence, brought laughter from the on lookers that had begun to gather. Still they hadn't finished.

'Right you are for it,' said the one not holding his face in his hand, followed quickly by, 'oh dear he has socked me in the eye now.'

He really had said that. All but over the man replaced his glasses and walked away. To return home to watch the highlights of the days football, to enjoy England's success or maybe Germany's defeat or possibly to mention to his wife the incident on his way home from town. Where he was set about by two figures from the past, emboldened by Pimms and Lemonade but still their fine breeding in place reluctant to hit a man wearing glasses, no matter how badly he may have deserved it.

Thirty Four - The Yorkshire Gentleman

The Cricket Season

'A fine day for it' the Yorkshire gentleman said, after his always polite good morning.

It was summer and the cricket season had begun. And being a Yorkshireman he would often refer to it during the purchase of his beers.

'A couple extra I think today,' he said placing eight small cans of Heineken on the counter, 'seeing as the cricket's on the telly.'

A two cans a day man, not a drinker, he would have enough now for the next three days plus a can or two to see him through the matches.

'And some peanuts to go with them,' he said preparing for his days viewing, 'my wife never took to it you know,' he said, more a statement than a question. 'Never understood it really, sport in general in fact,' he added 'truth be told. Snooker though,' he said shaking his head in mock bewilderment, 'snooker she adored. The only sport that she would be interested in, knew all the players, nicknames too. Where they came from, just about everything,' he said placing the Heineken in his shoulder bag. 'Hurricane this and whirlwind that and I don't know what else. Some fellow named Thorburn she was never keen on. Too slow for her. Ray Reardon though, she considered a gentleman. She liked him very much. I don't know, I really don't,' he added, making it clear that he was never that taken with Ray Reardon's charm. Or in fact the sport itself. 'Some Welsh chap, Terry somebody I think, I'm not sure. Had quite a thing for him though my wife. Not really a sport though is it I would say, pulling her leg and she would pretend to be annoyed at my cheek.'

As I handed him his change which he absent-mindedly took from me, I could see that his face had lit up as it always did when he spoke of his wife. Illuminated simply by recalling something she had said. Or a particular memory or an aspect of her personality.

'I always watched it though, the snooker,' he said patting his bag reassuringly, 'if it meant I would be in her company, a small sacrifice.' His eyes often red and a little watery were suddenly more so now. 'No sacrifice at all really,' he added before he bid me good day. And left with his cold beers to watch the game that he loved and his wife had never fully understood. To sit on his sofa a cold lager in front of him and peanuts too. Watching the cricket, absorbed in the snooker.

Thirty Five - Pauline

Being walked home

Pauline's visits to us were becoming less frequent with each month that passed and each time she seemed vaguer and more distant. She would still buy Harvey's Luncheon Dry but never these days wines to be shared with guests in her apartment building. She barely spoke when she came in. Her social skills now moved to auto pilot, remote control. Able to answer a direct question but almost incapable of offering a relevant point of view of her own aside from placing the order for her sherry. Having people 'round would only serve to unsettle her now and the balance of her environment.

Pauline stood immobile in front of the counter as I wrapped her sherry in tissue paper. Her body almost as impassive as her face now, waiting to be informed that the transaction was complete. Barely a part of it, not really involved at all. Pauline lived at Wyndham House, a warden controlled building of up-market apartments. We had spoken to the staff their regarding the sale of alcohol to Pauline. Did they feel that it in anyway compromised her safety? Should we perhaps for Pauline's sake stop serving her?

We liked Pauline, thought the world of her in fact. She had always been courteous and pleasant on her visits to us. And the last thing we wanted was to compromise her safety. We had spoken to the employees there and a member of the medical staff who visited the building and they had all said the same thing or roughly so. Pauline and others like her drew comfort from an evening drink. Her condition would not be affected by this, though her quality of life should it be removed would.

So Pauline got her sherry and I handed over her change and as had become customary she didn't move or make towards the door. She remained at the counter unsure of what to do next waiting for information, awaiting instructions.

After our meeting with the warden and the nurse we had begun walking Pauline home when she purchased her sherry. Locking up the shop for a few minutes to do so if alone on duty. I asked her if she would like to be shown home taking the shop keys from the till.

Pauline told me, 'That would be most kind,' and allowed me to walk her home.

Pauline no longer knew me or even fully recognised me now though I felt she trusted me. Perhaps it was instinct that told her she was safe, which told her she could trust me. Or more likely she no longer had any choice. Choice was for others now and was no longer something Pauline need concern herself with.

Thirty Six - The Students

Chelsea Clinton

Two men in dark suits entered the shop almost simultaneously. They took only a few steps inside, then positioned themselves either side of the door. They looked like well-dressed human bookends. They were in fact bodyguards for Chelsea Clinton.

She entered now as though coming in alone. The bodyguards did not acknowledge her but stood impassively neither frowning nor smiling. Chelsea said a polite 'hi' and began browsing amongst the Australian wines. She was by chance the only customer in the shop at this moment, I think by chance, but perhaps a third man was stationed outside preventing, politely I'm sure, anyone from entering until the president's daughter had made her purchase. She seemed quite happy though reading the labels and was left alone to make her choice. A student in a wine store, and for now, content to be just that.

After a few minutes she brought two bottles to the counter. One an Australian Shiraz, the other a Chardonnay, both four pounds and ninety nine pence. She looked about the shop as I took her payment in cash, said a warm thank you when the transaction was completed, smiled and left, closely followed by the bodyguards who simply nodded as they joined her. Their faces expressionless still and not a word spoken.

Chelsea Clinton, just a young girl doing what young girls do, buying wine for the weekend and staying within a student budget; two wines for under ten pounds. A young girl trying to appear normal, to be normal within the confines of a privileged life.

Thirty Seven - Charlie

Charlie and his Italian holiday

Charlie never bothered coming into the shop to announce his arrival. He simply pulled his truck alongside the building knowing in time that we would notice him. If he had to wait at all he would fill his time by organising the cases of wines and beers for our delivery. Stacking them at the side of the truck ready to be brought in when someone appeared. Sometimes if there was a delay in getting to him due to the shop being busy or answering the telephone, then Charlie would begin bringing in the goods himself, placing them in neat and ordered piles.

And familiar now with the layout he always knew where in the shop they needed to be put.

If the days order was small and his day was not a busy one Charlie would sit in the back of his lorry, watching people passing in the street. Filling his time waiting by drinking a Cola, or taking the opportunity to snack on a Cornish pasty or a pre-packed sandwich.

Charlie never drank at work. Those days were gone, along with the cigarettes, the mood swings, the antidepressants and the stress. The smoking and excessive drinking seemingly left behind with the keys to the pub he had managed. The stress had taken a little longer to shake off. But gone now, and the mood swings, the shouting and the aggressive behaviour directed at everyone including his wife thankfully passed too. Hazy now to Charlie as though these things were from a time thirty years ago. Or more recently but something that had happened to someone else,

someone that he had known but didn't like very much.
'Bon jorno,' Charlie said, handing me a case of Italian
wine, 'Come sta?'

Charlie liked to theme his banter according to the products
he was delivering and today's was made up almost entirely
of Italian wines and beers.

'We are off there this summer,' he said handing me a case
of Chianti, 'Tuscany and Umbria. Went there with my
wife when we had the pub,' he continued, 'we stayed for a
week and I can't remember a thing about it. I was off my
head at the time. My wife tells me it is very beautiful but
that I was not so beautiful, anything but in fact. Bit of a
nightmare apparently.'

He looked disappointed and stopped work for a moment. I
wondered if he was attempting to recall the holiday or
trying to keep it at bay.

Charlie was an intelligent man, well-educated and
interested in many things. Every now and again he would
mention something about Renaissance art or 18th century
poets or Russian artists. He would seldom continue for
long, mindful these days not to appear showy or worse still
to come across as the pub bore. He had been that before on
both sides of the bar. Nothing now would horrify him
more than to present himself as a self-important bore,
speaking but not listening, introducing subjects of
conversation seemingly at random, rambling at length
never bothering or interested enough to acknowledge
anyone's opinion but his own.

Charlie lost his disappointed look and smiled as he passed the wines. He told me that he and his wife would visit the monasteries of the area and the art galleries and museums all things they had done on their previous visit.

'Can't remember a sodding thing,' he said, 'I'll make it count now though and I'll make sure my wife enjoys herself this time around.'

Charlie passed me the final case of wine, 'I owe her that,' he said before closing up his lorry and climbing into the cab, 'and a fair bit more besides.'

'Chow, arriva-derci,' he said smiling as he pulled away. Thinking of his Italian holiday and looking out for his wife, eager to make amends and to make her feel special. And maybe, this time, they could both be special.

Thirty Eight - Ishmail

Serious Ishmail

Ishmail took drinking seriously, she never laughed or smiled. To her drinking was a serious business, an important undertaking and not one to be treated lightly. Sarcasm she could manage, or a withering smirk, but no laughter, no joy. Drinkers like Ishmail don't drink for pleasure. For her the purpose of drinking had nothing to do with fun. Drink for her had only one purpose, not to lighten the mood or to lessen inhibitions, not to stimulate or relax her, one purpose only. To get her as drunk as she was able and in the shortest time possible. Being drunk to Ishmail is the normal condition, any other to her is just time wasted.

Ishmail had progressed to a state of extreme alcoholism over a period of some five years. A casual drinker at first, then gradually less so, becoming more focused on volume and less intent on the flavour or the brand of her purchase. Her interest being solely its strength and its ability to get her intoxicated. Once pleasant enough, now rude and aggressive, paranoid and confused.

She has on occasion asked Yvonne, 'Where is Yvonne today?'

Only for Yvonne to answer, 'I have no idea Sir.'

Yvonne can be a little confused herself sometimes.

Finding out my surname Ishmail asked if I was her son, even though our names were not the same.

She once sidled up to a student quietly choosing wine and announced to his amazement that he was her husband. 'No

I am not,' he answered embarrassed.

'Aye ye are,' she said, 'you're my husband, bastard.'

We stopped serving Ishmail some years ago, and tried to explain why. However, being a paranoid alcoholic who exists entirely on short term memory, this has proved to be an incredibly difficult task. When refused service she would tell you that you had it wrong and that it wasn't her that was barred. Or she would say that was impossible as this was the first time in her life she had set foot in the place, adding, 'eejit.'

Or remembering that it was in fact not her first visit, she would say, 'that was ages ago,' and tell you not to be so 'stupit.'

She was right as it was now some two years since we had originally refused to serve her, but still she came in most weeks since that time. Each time she was as bewildered as the last and every time it seemed to Ishmail that she was being refused anew, wrongly denied, a case of mistaken identity. An innocent victim of conspiracy, which she could never fully understand.

Thirty Nine - Gary

Views on England

'Morning Gary,' I said trying to set an orderly tone.

'England, it's screwed,' he replied, making me wonder for a moment what I had actually said to him. 'Screwed,' he said again, not yet explaining how England had arrived at this sorry condition.

With Gary it could be anything; immigration, or as Gary would put it immigrants, or street crime, burglary, corrupt lawyers, politicians, unions, the NHS. He wasn't too keen on any of these and a few more besides.

'We were drowning a minute ago and now we are running out of water.'

Today it was to be the weather Gary was referring to. The floods and the drought that had followed. Gary gathered the things he would want for his lunch later, knowing the layout of the shop as well as I did. A packet of crisps or nuts, a chocolate bar or two from the display cabinet on the counter, a cold Coke Cola from the chiller by the window. And as he gathered he continued his theme,

'Place has had it, can't even water your garden now, hosepipe ban,' he said, stopping for a moment to catch my eye and to make sure that I was still with him.

'Die of thirst soon,' he said placing the litre bottle of coke on the counter.

Gary would like to leave England, he had said so many times, 'Get out before it sinks,' or 'before the whole place goes down the pan.'

Sometimes he would vary this to 'down the plughole' or 'down the drain' or sometimes 'goes to the dogs'. Though he had said on previous occasions that the country had already gone to the dogs. All the same he would like to leave England but was running out of places to go. Spain he no longer considered suitable believing the people there to be 'wankers'. Greece too had been removed from his list of possible options, due mainly to the lukewarm food and almost complete lack of sweet wine. Africa, India and Pakistan never stood a chance of hosting him in the first place.

'Thailand,' Gary said as he dropped his pile of crisps, nuts and chocolate bars on the counter, 'that would be all right. Some of the blokes go there,' he said jabbing a thumb towards the factory, 'cheap too and girls everywhere.' He stopped for a second and a concerned look came over him, 'Sometimes not even girls at all. Boys dressed up as girls. Lady-boys, sod that. Have to watch out for that especially on the lash.'

Ready to move on now his position on lady-boys clarified and the concerned expression gone from his face. Back to work, back to the factory to share his thoughts with his colleagues and no doubt to enlighten them as to the current condition of England, and the wayward ways of Thai boys masquerading as girls.

Forty - Adele

Adele and her sister

When Adele cried it was as though she cried the tears of a broken world. When she cried she rejected all physical support and was unhearing of any words of comfort or reassurance.

Adele was crying now, mascara and lipstick swirling on her face and mixing with the thick coating of foundation powder she always wore, making her appear at this moment unreal. Like a figure created by Picasso or Edvard Munch. Something other than human, less than human, and in the same instant more human than she had ever been.

Adele stood in front of the shelves stacked with lemonade, tonic and water and even now she still straightened the bottles. Separating tonic from bitter lemon and rearranging the bottles of water, assuring the sparkling water and the still water were not mixed together on the shelves.

Adele's sister had died recently bringing its own sadness and it was her sister who was responsible for today's tears. In good form for some time now constant in her mood. Neither high, which often she could be, or low, quiet and distant. She had only one sibling, her sister Sophie, like Adele born in France and sent to England at an early age. A job, a position and accommodation having been arranged for her. Adele loved and trusted her sister supporting her emotionally, though fragile enough herself, and financially when she was in need, which seemed to be most of the time.

Finished now with the bottles of water, Adele took another tissue from the pocket of the apron she always wore at work. She blew her nose and wiped her eyes but still the tears came. Her main compass of hurt seemed to be the fact that her sister had lied and manipulated her for much of her life.

'She tricked me,' she said between sobs, 'and for so long.' She had told me in a surprisingly calm way that her sister was in fact wealthy beyond her understanding. When the will was read it transpired that she owned the house in Norwich that she and her daughter had lived in for so long. It wasn't rented or subsidised by the council as she had been led to believe. It was hers, and now the house and the money in the bank along with the investments and a pension added up to many hundreds of thousands of pounds. Adele had said that she had no interest in the house or the money and that it was, 'now only right and proper' that it should go to her sister's only daughter, but why, she asked, did she feel the need to lie to her, manipulate and trick her. Making her a fool, 'A gullible fool,' were the words she had actually used.

I offered to take her home to rest and to cry, or perhaps she would like to sit upstairs for a while. But she did not respond and I did not press the issue. Sometimes I could not fathom Adele, her silences or her highs. I loved her though and longed to help her. And today I understood why she cried her tears of a broken world.

All that she held dear was shattered the best and most constant thing in her life was a sham. Her sister and the love and trust she believed they had shared were gone. In fact it had never really existed in the first place.

'Well,' she said suddenly, her crying all but over as quickly and surprisingly as it had begun, 'there is work to be done my dear. Just give me a moment.'

When she returned from the cloakroom a few minutes later her face had been cleaned and her make-up and lipstick had been reapplied. And though her eyes were red and half closed like a boxer in the latter part of a long and hard fight there were no sign of tears.

Adele finished her shift working quietly and diligently as she always did. She ignored all future attempts to talk of her sister refusing to acknowledge any mention of her. And I never heard her speak her sister's name again.

Forty One - Angie

The quiet nurse

Angie, as far as I was aware, had never called into the shop on her own. Always accompanied by a friend who lived locally or a visitor from out of town.

One or two of the restaurants in our neighbourhood operated a bring your own policy regarding wines and beers. Some Indian owned restaurants unwilling to sell alcohol out of respect and adherence to their religion. It was good for us, good for trade; also it often introduced new customers who otherwise might not know of the store's existence.

This night Angie was standing silently at the counter while her friend down from London paid for their wine. I knew Angie vaguely. One of her friends was seeing a friend of mine, like all towns, a village really. I had met her once briefly at their place and I knew that she was a nurse. I asked her how she was and where they were heading.

'The Bombay,' she said referring to a nearby restaurant, 'I'm fine though,' she added seeming to realise that she hadn't answered the enquiry regarding how she was.

'A curry,' she added, referring to the wine and smiling I thought a little shyly.

She was looking down at the floor now and had fallen strangely silent. I wondered if I had offended her in some way or intruded upon their evening.

'Enjoy your meal,' I said finally, directing my words towards her London friend.

'Oh we will,' her friend said, 'we both love Indian food don't we Angie?'

Then they left and I began serving another customer.

As I did so I briefly wondered if they would have a good time. But of course they would, two old friends talking over a curry and a glass or two of wine to get them chatting, what could be better.
The woman down from London and her quiet friend with the shy smile and a love of Indian cuisine.

Forty Two - The Author

The author

No one as far as I was aware really knew if he was a writer. Local people said that he had had many books published but nobody seemed to have come across any, or overly troubled themselves attempting to do so. Still he was known by all as the author. A heavy drinker, whisky, always it was whisky, and usually intoxicated to one degree or another no matter what time of day he called in. He rarely spoke except for the few words needed to place his order. There was no necessity even for these. More a courtesy on both parts, a polite interaction.

Two bottles of house whisky, Claymore, every day. In addition to his frequent visits to various public houses dotted about the city. No trouble in those places and no trouble to us. Polite in a quiet way, humble even. He was well spoken, his voice soft and gentle though sometimes slurred and often hoarse.

This day when he called in for his whisky his winter coat was more shabby than usual. Crumpled and dirty as though he had taken to sleeping in it. He was unshaven, unkempt and more vague and distracted than was usual. Though he always seemed preoccupied and distant. He asked for his usual two bottles of whisky and not for the first time I wondered if I should decline to serve him but on what grounds? On what authority, moral or otherwise? Refuse him because he had forgotten how to use a razor or a toothbrush. Because his coat was matted and creased. Because the whisky would take its toll, would in time impair and eventually destroy his organs and corrode a brain that had been possibly, was still, very sharp, though clearly already slowed and damaged.

He paid me for the whisky and I handed him the bag in which I had placed the bottles. The transaction successfully completed for another day he left the shop walking slowly, stooped and almost shuffling to return to a smart riverside cottage bought from the proceeds of his books, or possibly to a small room on the top floor of a Victorian terraced house. Bereft of food and of comfort to open another bottle of whisky and who could know perhaps to continue work on his latest novel, something grand, poetic, articulate and beautiful. To say the things that he needed to say, to find the words to put down on paper where so few were actually spoken.

Forty Three - Gary

Canteen food

Gary comes in most lunch times. He could eat in the canteen at work if, 'The food wasn't so shit. Expect us to eat that. It's a fucking insult.'

Usually Gary buys a packet of crisps, sometimes two. Walker's cheese and onion are his favourite.

'Really pisses the blokes off when I breathe on them.'

Also a Mars bar, a Topic and a packet of Scampi Fries just to top up his breath. All washed down by a litre bottle of Coca Cola.

Gary likes to get out of the factory for a bit at lunchtime. It's healthier and anyway, he 'wouldn't insult a dog with that crap.'

Forty Four - Karen

The delivery woman

Karen was very private, but sometimes she would open up, a bit. She delivered to us usually once a week and though she liked a joke and a chat, still she kept her private life to herself. On being asked if she'd had a good weekend – Karen delivered on a Monday- she would normally keep her answers polite but general.

'No not really,' she would say due to the 'pissing rain' or that they had not done much really. Today was different.

'We went on a bit of a bender,' she said, 'well he did anyway, sodding men,' she added as though I wasn't of that gender.

'He's ok most of the time,' her bloke and he had managed to stay in work for a good while now.

'It's the drink. He starts Friday afternoon and carries on until he passes out on Sunday night. He's usually ok though, not normally nasty, not normally violent.' she said trying to smile. 'Kicked me' she added, 'he's never done that before, never kicked me.'

I'd seen bruising on Karen's arms before at times as we had unloaded her lorry. But assumed they were due to nothing more sinister than the lifting of heavy cases of wine and crates of spirits.

'Probably something stupid I'd said, something that annoyed him. He'll be all right tonight, better than being on your own,' she said stacking cases of wine now, 'I hate being on my own.'

Forty Five - Alex

The drunks

Alex wasn't part of a street gang as such, not officially or in a recognised way. Rarely though on his own, usually accompanied by at least two or three other street drinkers, ragged and unkempt his companions, as he himself was. Mostly they were men rather than teenagers, hard men probably in their time. Alex I would have guessed to be in the region of 35 or 40 years of age, but it was difficult to be exact. The greying beard prematurely aged him as did his lined skin, damaged by the elements. Aged also by his constant alcohol consumption, Alex seemingly would drink most things; sherry, cider, strong lager, brandy, anything, though Special Brew seemed to be his drink of choice when choice was available to him. We had stopped serving Alex some months back, his behaviour becoming increasingly aggressive and erratic. Often now though he would stand off down the road, out of sight and get someone else to buy the drink for him. At these times he was no trouble to us. Obtaining his beers or his sherry and discreetly drinking himself into a stupor before falling asleep somewhere, on the meadow or in a park.

Today though was different. Over the shoulder of the customer I was serving, I could see Alex. He was standing just inside the doorway.

'I want beer,' he was saying, his body language threatening and his eyes wide with alcohol and aggression, 'I want beer,' he said again as the customer I had now

finished serving moved past him and left the shop.
I moved from behind the counter in an attempt to usher
him from the store, reminding him as I did so, that he no
longer got served here. Some of the street drinkers, usually
the younger ones, would often supplement their drinking
with something else; cannabis, heroin or amphetamine
which was popular too, due to its availability and low cost.
Alex was dribbling from the corners of his mouth so that a
white froth had formed on either side of his beard.
Probably speeding too, I thought.
He was on his own today which was unusual, though I was
relieved to see that he was. I wondered as I attempted to
direct him out of the door if his erratic and aggressive
behaviour had scared off his drinking companions.
I mentioned something about calling the police, something
we never liked to do and also used the threat sparingly as a
last resort. At times the mentioning of the police could
have a calming effect. But often it could have quite the
opposite reaction, only managing to inflame the situation,
raising it to a new and barely manageable level.
Alex began ranting now, telling me that I was 'a dead
man,' threatening my family, my friends, the premises.
Words and obscenities erupting from him as I led him
through the door.
I had heard that Alex had formally been an army man,
which as is the way of such rumours had been elevated to
a member of the S.A.S.
I doubted that, but the former could well have been true.
He was powerfully built, even now, in spite of his lifestyle,
and I had no doubt he was capable of extreme violence
when the need and the circumstances required him to be.

I stood in front of him now and as I blocked the entrance I thought I could detect the smell of petrol coming from him. It may have been brandy or stale lager or urine, possibly a heady chemical blending of them all. Probably not fuel at all, nothing to do with petrol this smell. All the same, for a brief moment I imagined the premises ablaze late at night, and Alex walking away that cunning look on his face, pleased with his night's work and the horror he had left in its wake.

Then as we stood on the step outside the door, Alex turned and began to walk away.

'I want fucking beer,' he said as he went, less forceful now, beginning to accept there was nothing for him here. He gained speed, still muttering abuse, walking away from the shop. Walking faster than a drunken man had a right to walk, to try his luck elsewhere.

'Fucking piece of shit!' he shouted as he went further down the road then finally out of sight.

I went back inside the shop. There would be no point calling the police, what could I tell them anyway. He hadn't broken or stolen anything, or physically assaulted me. My hands shook as I served the next customer to come in and I struggled to operate the keys of the till.

The voice I heard emanating from me as I served the young, well dressed, polite student was not my own. What could I tell the police? That he had scared me? His reputation, the abuse, the wild unpredictable look in his eyes. I had been frightened in a way that at one time I would not have been.

Alex and others like him try to get their way by attrition, a gradual wearing down, until for some it is easier to give in and let them have their way and serve them, sometimes even giving them beers and ciders for free in exchange for not causing problems for them or their premises or for their loved ones. Food too from restaurants and cafés given, often free. Not as an act of compassion rather though as an admission of defeat. An acceptance, a recognition of the fact that Alex, all the Alex's would just keep pushing, would just continue to come until finally it was easier to give in.

The police, overworked and understaffed could, even with the best will, do little. Phone them up, ring 999 and tell them that my hands were still shaking and that I probably would not sleep that night. Tell them that though nothing had been stolen or broken, I was finding it difficult to use the till. Tell them that once again in something as mundane as the work place I had been made to know fear, and each time it happened the fear became greater.

How could I tell them? How could I explain that to the police, admit that to anyone when I was finding it so difficult, impossible really to admit it, even to myself.

Forty six - Gary

The BBQ

Gary was planning a barbeque at the weekend, or rather his parents were. Gary lives with his mum and dad. 'If the weather holds up, can't plan a funeral in this country, never mind a BBQ. Screwed up place.'
Gary was looking at wines in the bargain buckets. Liebfraumilch at two ninety nine had caught his eye. 'Why can't they put it in English?' he asked, 'Haven't they caused enough trouble?'
Gary knew this wine and though not best pleased with its place of origin, still deemed it to be, 'frigging all right.'
He placed his order for the barbeque, a dozen bottles would 'be good' and a case of Stella. I told him there would be a discount as it was a fair sized order.
'Not bothered,' he answered, 'the old man's paying for it. He's got loads. Might rain though, probably will. I'll bring it back if it does.'
The weekend was sunny. Gary and his mum and dad and their friends had a good time and they enjoyed the wine very much.
'My mum liked it a lot. Not bad for kraut juice,' she said, 'fucking funny that.'
Gary was still laughing at his mother's comments as he left the shop. She's a 'gem' his mum he had mentioned that before and 'priceless' and 'top quality'. 'Best mum in the world', all that and a stand-up comedian too. He is a lucky man Gary to have a mum like that. He would tell you so himself and would need very little by way of

encouragement to do just that.

Forty Seven - Sylvia and Peter

Not so dusty

Sylvia used an expression that I have never heard anyone else use. On being asked how she was, she would sometimes reply 'not so dusty', and though she would say it in a light hearted, cheerful manner, I felt she used it on days when she was anything but light hearted. It was the vocal equivalent of putting on a brave face. A standard response that created a little distance between her and the person she was communicating with. A technique designed to keep interactions light and impersonal when the need arose.

On days such as this, Sylvia would keep things brief. Peter was a bit under the weather, she said though there was no need for her to explain anything. They had called the doctor out for the last two nights.

Many years ago Peter had built coffins for Sylvia and himself. Beautiful things, Sylvia had mentioned before, made of fine oak and the workmanship and the finish was wonderful. Peter was as good with his hands as he was with his brain. A rare enough thing the combination of the two. But not something Peter was boastful about. Or possibly even aware of.

Sylvia had mentioned the coffins many times over the years. Laughing and joking when speaking of them. Not something connected with loss or with loneliness, but something quite humorous, something amusing that was made all the more so being that the coffins were stored beneath their bed, 'a good wheeze' in fact.

As Peter's inevitable time of passing grew nearer however, Sylvia mentioned the coffins less and less. Then she spoke of them not at all. It is easy to laugh when death is a distant, half imagined thing. A ghostly shadow, a spectre that stalked other people not you; older people, or the sick or the infirm.

Something had affected Sylvia last night, 'Bothered me,' she said, 'a small thing.'

Thinking he was alone in their room, apart from Peter resting, the Doctor had taken a look at the coffins laying beneath the bed. Peter, sleeping would not have noticed this. Sylvia saw it though, this interest from the Doctor, a brief assessment. And though it was a small thing, a glance really, still it had kept her awake for most of the night. She had to leave the shop now. There were some things she needed to buy from the supermarket. Sylvia knew so many people here. And no doubt she would reply to their greeting with a cheery 'not so dusty'. It wasn't true though that response. I think Sylvia was very dusty today, very dusty indeed.

Forty Eight - Craig Rhaine

The poet

It had just passed closing time, when he and a friend came into buy a bottle of malt whisky. Closing time is a difficult time for a wine store. The risk of being robbed is at the highest for the entire twenty four hour period. Less people around, and cashing up the till which is at its fullest, or money on the premises at least. The takings having reached their maximum now. Also other shops which may close earlier create a knock on effect. Customers whom those shops would normally service would look elsewhere for that last minute bottle of wine, cans of lager, or in this case a bottle of malt whisky to round off an evening.

I liked Craig Rhaine's poetry. In particular I liked *A Martian Sends A Postcard Home*. A clever take on how a species from another planet would view us. The key had been in the door when he and his friend had entered, of course we would serve him. We would always serve late customers unless they were drunk or quarrelsome. If they could just be fairly quick though, they were told then that would be appreciated. They began looking at the long row of malts on offer. Outside I could see that some of the more unpleasant drunks had begun to gather. Many of the other shops closed now, as we normally would be. Craig Rhaine was discussing in depth with his friend the various characters of the malts on offer. Smokey over light, an aroma of peat was good for him as was a suggestion of woodland oak.

The drunks outside were becoming more daring. The shop
lights still on and customers standing at the counter. We
were obviously open for trade and that may even apply to
the violent element amongst them. Even those previously
refused would now begin to think that those rules, along
with the normal time of closing no longer existed.
It was clear, by now that the poet chose his whisky with
the same precision with which he chose his words.
Smiling, as he scanned the shelf and intelligent and warm.
No doubt helped by the warmth of a few ales at the Turf
Tavern, Judd the Obscure or maybe The Eagle and Child.
He was surprised when I hurried him, asked him if it was
possible that they could make their choice. It was now well
past closing time. I hadn't intended to sound sharp, though
I suspect that I did. The tension rising in me now, when
first the swimming head of one drunk and then another
appeared inside the door. I hurried the poet again at the
same time informing the drunks that we were closed. A
pack mentality was clearly forming. An opportunity which
they had not expected had arisen. If they got inside, if they
entered on masse, at this time of night and with a full days
alcohol inside them, there would be chaos.
I pushed the poet further insisting now that we needed to
close and that he must make a choice.
He pointed to a bottle of twelve year old Glenmorangie,
'That please,' was all he said.
I took the money and bagged the whisky as swiftly as
possible. The transaction over, he was oblivious to the
drunks. They were not after all any of his concern,
noticing only my perceived rudeness. I know I had ruined
that moment for him. The pleasure involved in choosing,

as great as the aroma, its colour in a glass or its taste when reaching the palate. All diminished now. The ritual spoiled by the need for haste.

The drunks had entered the shop but this seemed to go unnoticed by him as he left. They were in now and he was gone, annoyed and confused, perhaps even hurt. I wonder what his Martian would have made of the way he was treated. I doubt he would have been too impressed.

Forty Nine - Gary

Screw 'em

Gary was always at his best on a Monday. He'd had the weekend to read the papers.

'No, screw them,' he said, a slight variation on his previous greeting, 'It's all wrong and we're paying for it too.'

He fell silent for a moment or two as he undertook the ritual of choosing his lunch.

'I'll tell you why we're paying,' he said, though I hadn't directly asked him as I was behind with a wine order, 'because they tell us too that's why. Idiots.'

Gary left now. He was in a hurry as he needed to buy something from the bike shop before returning to work.

'All wrong,' he repeated as he left to find an inner tube or a lamp for his bike.

'They must think we're stupid,' he finished with, before heading for the bike shop.

What was all wrong? I wondered as I tried to finish the order. What is it that we're paying for but probably shouldn't be? And most importantly who is it that Gary says we are supposed to screw.

Fifty - The Spies

Part one

A man in an expensive looking business suit was browsing in the shop. When you work with the public on a regular basis you develop an instinct for unusual behaviour. Something like an antenna or an alarm. Shoplifters need to be looked out for or potential troublemakers. Also it is necessary in a non-intrusive way to be mindful of someone who may need assistance in choosing a wine to go with fish or lamb or beer to compliment Indian food or a beef casserole.

With his smart grey shirt, matching tie and immaculately cut hair he would have seemed quite at home in London's Canary Wharf. Bells were beginning to chime.

'What's this like,' he asked, picking up a bottle of Cotes Du Rhone from one of the display bins. He was told that it was a medium to full bodied red, a little spicy and good value having won a silver medal award from 'International Wine Magazine'.

'Really,' he said, seeming unwilling to accept some or all of the information. The rosette from the wine magazine was attached to the card on the basket with a description of the wine and the price. 'Really,' he said again, 'for 3.99?' Clearly unconvinced he put the wine back in the basket. 'But what's it like?' he asked again.

Not knowing what more he needed, I simply said that it was a very nice wine. He continued to circle the shop appearing to be unsure whether he was buying wine, malt whisky, vodka, beer or even bottled water. Picking up bottles of San Perigino or Tsing Tao Beer from China or a relatively obscure bottled ale from Cumbria or Cornwall. He asked about the malt whiskys we stocked and could he look at one or two of our Havana rums. He checked out the crisps and nuts and he asked about the draft beer. What do we dispense it into, the price and so on.

One of things we tried to specialise in was takeaway draught ale. On one of the counters which had in fact been a bar from a pub that had closed down, there were four traditional beer handles. Beer engines they were called. They were connected to various barrels of beer kept in the cellar below the shop. We would draw up the beer into 4 pint containers or 8 pint or even into 36 pint take away casks. For parties and such like, it was very popular and customers seemed to enjoy its relative novelty. As well as stocking bottled beers and wines that the big chain off-licences and supermarkets did not stock, it was something we offered as a unique service in the area and something that helped us to be a little different and to stay in business. Finished now with the draught ale he seemed satisfied with his tour of the shop.

'I'll take one of your very nice award winning Cotes Du Rhones,' he said, looking extremely self satisfied as though he had managed a joke and a put-down all in one go.

We often had people from other stores or pubs maybe, looking around the place to see what we were selling that they were not. Everybody did it, including us. We called them 'spies'. We didn't really bother about it that much. But this had felt different. More than a visit from a local rival, more calculating and sinister than that.

The man in the sharp suit paid me and looked about the shop one final time as he left.

'Spy,' Adele would have said in a stage whisper, loud enough for all to hear. And she would have been right. Later we were to hear that he was in fact a business consultant from one of the biggest breweries in the country. They were in the process of branching out from the pub trade and had already opened a string of pub themed wine and beer superstores in London and Manchester. Oxford was next and the premises for which they had applied for a licence was in the same road as us, a huge, sprawling place. Big enough to unbalance a neighbourhood. A vast drinks outlet appearing the middle of a close knit community. Big enough also to put us out of business and corporate enough not to care.

Fifty One - Spies

The sequel

The next time I saw the man in the expensive suit was in the Magistrates Court in the centre of the city. The suit had changed, dark blue now though it looked every bit as expensive as the previous one. I would have known him though no matter what he was wearing by the self-assured expression that seemed to be fixed permanently to his face. We were here to oppose the Licence application that he and his team were applying for. Many people, local people from our part of town filled the room.

The room was large and bright, full of the subdued clatter of footsteps echoing on tiles, chairs being adjusted and the occasional cough or nose being blown. Some people smiled as we entered, reassuring smiles, in the main from people we knew well, mostly at least. It was our job with the help of a barrister to oppose the licence and if possible to have the application denied. The local residents would try to assist us in that. They had no desire for a drinks superstore in the midst of their small community. Also I believed they were here, some of them at least in support of us. The man in the sharp suit whose name I now knew. The licence was to be in his name as someone has to be individually responsible for the licence to sell alcohol. It needed to be granted to a person not a company, however large that company was. Care must be taken not to serve people already intoxicated or supply under-age teenagers with alcohol. Though young people have ways of obtaining things that they should not obtain. Often ingenious ways. And alcohol in our society was one of those things.

I knew that at some point I would be called to the stand, to give my reasons as to why this licence should not be granted. My barrister had made it clear that we could not oppose it on the grounds that it may put us out of business. In a free, democratic, capitalist world that stood for nothing.

Amongst the people 'on our side' were many familiar faces, Sylvia, though without Peter, too frail now to be directly involved in a day like this. A day which promised to be long and tiring. Sylvia, win or lose would tell him all about it later. Sharing her involvement and her observations so that he would barely have missed a thing. The landlord of a local pub, a journalist that lived in the area and did not want it to change, the owners of the local delicatessen and a representative from the old people's home which lay to the rear of the proposed superstore. People that I knew personally and by name and some simply by sight all against the granting of the licence. Though our barrister had told them that it was highly unlikely that we would be successful in this and that in some twenty years, he had personally never known a licence to be refused.

Representing the brewery was an entire team made up of barristers, expert witnesses and the company accountant. Immaculately turned out in dark well-made suits. Emanating success, opulence and even power.

I was pleased with the turn out from 'our side' though, proud that they cared enough about their lives and where they lived them to attend. And as the magistrates entered to take their places on the bench I felt for a moment, that whatever the outcome we were in this together. Though we had more to lose than most; our livelihoods and everything involved with that.

Fifty Two - Spies

The conclusion

Many people were called to speak that day in court. Though I believe that two things in particular influenced the outcome. The first was Bill.

Bill was the spokesman for the local residents home for the elderly. Well into his seventies now, though still in full command of body and of mind. Bill said his piece when called to the stand, giving his reasons for being against the proposed wine superstore. All the residents of the home were opposed to it and every one of them had signed a petition confirming this. Bill had held this petition in his hand as he spoke or answered the questions put to him by the company's barrister. He had stated that they did not see the need for yet another place selling alcohol.

'There's enough boozing all ready,' was how he put it. Also they felt, the residents, that it would bring a rowdy element to the street in which they lived and to the community itself. Making their way from the town centre, teenage drinkers and students drinking more than they should. And more than safely they could. Bill finished by saying he had seen the problems that such an outlet could bring in other places he had lived. And that they, the residents of the home, were in fact scared.

'Frightened,' he said, of youthful drunken gangs roaming the streets and terrorising the people that lived there. Scared too of street drinkers begging aggressively, intimidating them and making them fearful to venture out of their building. The barrister said something about this being a vast exaggeration based on very little real evidence. But still the damage had been done and Bill's point had been raised.

I could see Sylvia smiling as Bill left the stand. Many others too seemed pleased with Bill and with the way he had conducted himself. Also there was the proposed licensee, the original spy and purchaser of award winning Cotes Du Rhone. The wine in his estimation that couldn't possibly be worth buying due to its low cost. He was confident on the stand and spoke eloquently and at length of the need to provide an area with the widest possible choice. He spoke of wines that they would sell and exotic beers or spirits. Most of which we already sold. He spoke of the parking area which would attract 'numbers' from a large catchment area. He explained the need for just such an enterprise in this 'district'. And he referred to the area by its postcode at all times. Never once did he call it a community or mention people or residents or their individual needs. To him it seemed there were no people involved in this. No human aspect whatsoever, simply a postcode.

After many hours of hearing witness statements from both sides and after long deliberation by the magistrates to our surprise and great relief the application was denied. We were never fully to know the reasons the licence was refused though we would question and guess amongst ourselves. The people and the community in which they lived would stay unchanged, for the time being at least. And we, with their help and only with their help, would remain in business.

Fifty Three - Karen

Delivery men and women

Karen joked as she handed me down the cases of Stella from her truck. She was talkative today, and smiling as she went about her work. Though to me she seemed irritable, which wasn't like her.

'The last ten days have been hard,' she said, 'work-wise that is,' she added.

There was an international football tournament taking place. According to Karen the whole world has gone 'football crazy' including 'her bloke.'

'And lager crazy too,' she said her smile gone now, 'ten days he's been on the piss,' referring again to 'her bloke'.

'Wanker!' she spat out, passing the cases of Stella faster and faster as she spoke, 'Ten days sitting in front of the box drinking this. Shouts and fucking swears at me no matter what team wins.'

Karen apologised for 'her French'. I'd never heard her swear before.

'Even worse if the wrong team wins. Chucked him out on Sunday,' she said, stopping for a moment to raise her sweatshirt revealing bruising around the ribs, 'I think he would have killed me when England got knocked out. It would have been my fault, somehow.'

Karen was adamant that this was it and that she would not have him back, not this time.

'Can't be frightened of someone who's supposed to love you, can you? Sod him.'

She looked confident, as though she really meant it.

'Sod him,' she said again 'fucking waste of space, excuse my French.'

Fifty Four - Charlie

Charlie and the Beaujolais

Charlie was here for the second time this week. One delivery a week from his company was usually sufficient. This week was different however, Charlie had a second delivery.

Today was Beaujolais Nouveau day and Charlie had three pallets of it for us. The Beaujolais is only released on a certain day, the same for everyone, be it restaurant, bar or wine shop. Released at midnight in France to start a stampede of excitement and competition to see who and where in each area could have it available first. At this time and from the late eighties pubs and restaurants would seek special licences from the local authorities. These licences would allow them to open early, sometimes as early as six or seven a.m. to offer Beaujolais Nouveau breakfasts, sausages, bacon, eggs and great spreads of Camembert and Brie, fresh French bread and olives accompanied of course by huge amounts of the raw, underdeveloped and un-aged red wine.

Charlie had two pallets for us, such was its popularity and so great was its demand. Charlie got it though, 'A market driven con,' he said, sliding his hand operated forklift beneath the first pallet of Nouveau, 'more expensive than the real stuff and no comparison on quality. Fun though,' he added, 'may as well go with it.'

He went on to say that he was taking his wife out to dinner this evening somewhere nice he said and 'we'll be drinking some of this too.'

Charlie carried on chatting as he unloaded the wine saying that he and his wife were back on track and that they had so nearly lost it, 'I nearly lost it. I can't believe we came so close to splitting up,' he said, pausing for a moment for an almost theatrical shake of the head. It wasn't theatrical though that expression, or even funny, so real to him, so horrendous the possibility of losing his wife that it could not be a subject for humour.

I had to leave Charlie for a moment to answer the telephone. A few minutes later when I returned he was out of his reverie and whistling cheerfully as he stacked the boxes.

'You ok?' he asked, 'you look a bit funny.'

I told him I was fine then went on to say that I thought I had just been asked out on a date.

'Fair play,' said Charlie, 'must be the Beaujolais or something in the air. Rascal,' he said winking at me as he said it.

He meant me I am sure with his rascal comment, though he could just as well have been referring to the quiet nurse. The quiet nurse with the shy smile and the courage to ask someone out because she said she knew that if we met properly and spent some time together we would get on so well.

'Rascal,' Charlie repeated and I could not help but agree with him. Rascal indeed, and maybe not so quiet after all.

Fifty Five - The Old Boxer

Round one

We never really found out if he had been a boxer or not. And though he would raise his fists in the way that Irishman outside pubs at closing time are prone to doing, we never actually saw him throw a punch. His body language was meant to imply that he was primed and willing to beat the bejesus out of anyone and everyone at a moment's notice.

'I fought Gipsy John Francome himself,' he was fond of saying, 'and he didn't have it all his own way I can tell you.'

Once he began a rant it was difficult to stop him. So we tried to serve him quickly but not too quickly as this was often taken by him as curt, or rude, or even confrontational. Serve him and say a polite thank you which was often enough to prompt the old boxer to realise the transaction was complete. He had got what he came for and now it was time to leave. Never though ever, and not even a hand on his shoulder whilst coaxing him towards the door touch him. Not so much as hand on the shoulder or a finger placed upon his arm. If you did it was as though a bell had been rung to commence a bout. Seconds out, round one. He would instantly take up his boxing stance with his hands up and animated now and all the time he would be reminding you not to even think about laying a hand on him. And that in fact he could beat six of you and that would be on a bad day. Also during the rant he would say he had fought men bigger than you, tougher than you and he was sure smarter than you. One such man presumably being Gipsy John Francome, Gipsy John Francome himself.

Fifty Six - The Complainers

Mr H

Complaining seemed to be Mr H's natural form of expression. Almost everything he spoke of or commented on had a negative position. Today the weather was 'far too warm' and he observed the pollen count must be 'through the roof'.

It was always a good place to start for Mr H, the weather. Direct enough to elicit if not deserve a response. While being valid, this being England, for an unfavourable comment or two in the cause of choosing his purchase which he seemed to be in the process of doing. He picked up a bottle of Bordeaux and returned it almost immediately to the shelf, his features mildly contorted. A vague expression of displeasure on his face. Something about the wine was not to his liking. The price perhaps, or the year, or the design of the label maybe. Who could know? I asked him if he needed any assistance to which he replied a little forcefully,

'Certainly not.'

I decided to busy myself until Mr H was ready to make his purchase. He had deserted the French wines for now and had unexpectedly began foraging in one the beer chillers. Moving the bottles of Becks, and Sol and Grolsch, picking them up and holding them before putting them back in the chiller. I couldn't help noticing that on a few occasions he held a beer to his cheek before returning it to the cabinet.

'Too cold,' he said closing the doors. 'These beers are far too cold.'

It was, as he himself had stated, a warm day, and it could be considered that a cold beer would be a good thing.

'And these are far too warm,' he said referring to the bottles of beers on the shelf, 'I don't suppose I have any choice,' he said, taking a single bottle of Becks from the shelf and placing it on the counter.

'I'll have to cool it to the correct temperature at home and I had rather hoped to drink it immediately considering the heat of the day.'

Mr H paid for his beer, his one warm unsatisfactory beer and headed out of the shop. Into the sunshine to traipse home. A disappointed, disgruntled figure hot and thirsty and now thanks to us he would have to wait until his beer had cooled sufficiently before he could enjoy it. As I checked the temperature of the cold beers, I couldn't help but think that enjoyment was something that Mr H had seldom been overly familiar with.

Fifty Seven - Pauline

Do you know me?

Increasingly Pauline's features failed to register emotion, her face 'masked' now. Today though, as she entered the shop, she was different. Her face was still devoid of expression but in her eyes there was anxiety and confusion.

I greeted her wishing her a good morning, as much in an attempt to put her at her ease as one of courtesy and I spoke her name as I did so.

'Do you know me?' she asked, reacting to the use of her name. Surprise now briefly replacing anxiety.

'Yes Pauline,' I answered, 'I know you, everyone here knows you.'

Pauline had been calling into the store two or three times a week since moving to the area, three years ago. She would buy wine for guests or dry sherry as a pleasant nightcap for herself. She must have visited us more than two hundred times.

'You know me?' she said again, attempting to grasp something of the situation, trying to locate some strand of familiarity. A voice she recognised or a face that she knew.

'Then,' she said, 'could you possibly tell me where I live.'

After initial reassurances that Pauline seemed disinterested in, or more probably unable to fully register, she was taken home, home to where she lived now. You could almost see her building on stepping out of the shop door. We walked mainly in silence, she seemed more comfortable this way and less confused. And besides what was there really to say. Her interest now was purely about reaching home, and being amongst familiar things. The entire sum of her focus based solely on that one thing. She could have been accompanied by a murderer or a rapist, so vulnerable she was, but that did not enter into her reckoning. It was of no concern to her. She had her hands full simply trying to take hold of and to grasp something of this moment. The past was gone now, the majority of it at least and the future beyond her reckoning or her consideration.

'I know this place,' she said as we approached her building, 'I will be fine now, thank you, thank you so much.'

Pauline who had no interest now in the food that she ate or the colour of the sky. Books or films or TV no longer a part of her world and people too becoming less relevant with every day that passed. Still now she had her manners, still she was polite and courteous.

'You have been most kind,' she said again. Force of habit that had been employed and honed throughout a lifetime. Pauline was 'home' to her warden controlled accommodation. A building designed less for living than to be functional. To be a place of safety within its limitations. Fast now becoming insufficient for Pauline's increasing need for care. Unable to provide her with the degree of vigilance she would require to help her maintain something so assumed by all of us as the awareness of personal safety. That fundamental element of function having all but deserted her. Her independence gone for this lifetime, it was time for Pauline to move on.

Fifty Eight - Gary and Ishmail

The ditch and the brandy

'I know that old girl,' Gary said placing a newspaper on the counter, 'she's from 'round here,' he added, before beginning the process of choosing his lunch from a wine store.

The newspaper Gary had brought in was the early addition of the Oxford Mail, a local tabloid consisting more of adverts and motor car supplements than of hard hitting news stories.

The 'old girl' that Gary was referring to was Ishmail, serious Ishmail. Staring out from the newspapers front page with the headline - 'Elderly woman found alive after two nights in a freezing ditch.'

According to the article Ishmail had become disorientated on leaving a pub at closing time and had begun walking in the wrong direction. Confused and a little worse for wear, Ishmail had sat down at the side of the road, to take stock and get her bearings. Somehow she had failed to notice the space she had chosen to rest at was in fact the side of a ditch. She had fallen in and remained there for 2 days and 2 nights.

The article praised her fortitude and her unwavering spirit, pointing out that Ishmail was in her sixties and adding helpfully that November was not the best time to take up residence in a roadside ditch.

Ishmail was quoted as saying that at first she had shouted and wailed and then she must have fallen asleep. When she awoke it was daylight and she shouted and wailed again.

When no one came she opened the half bottle of brandy she had purchased before leaving the pub the previous evening. She drank some brandy, shouted for help and when no one came, she fell back to sleep again. This pattern she repeated over and over until eventually someone heard her cries and called for an ambulance. Understandably, the article continued Ishmail made little sense regarding her ordeal. Though she did say ,
'People have been telling me for ages to stop the drinking. Saved my life that brandy,' she added, forgetting to mention that it was brandy that had endangered her life in the first place.
'Lucky for me I had it on me, eejits,' she had said, holding up the empty bottle and presenting the newspaper photographer with an unmissable, if slightly staged photo opportunity accompanied by the caption 'Brandy keeps 68 year old alive for two nights in freezing ditch.'
'Tough old bird,' pronounced Gary as he gathered his off-licence lunch and rolled up his newspaper.
'Lucky for her that she'd bought that brandy. She would have died of hypothermia or something else without it,' he said as he left.
For once I agreed with Gary, though I did wonder what the 'something else' would have been if the hypothermia hadn't got her first.

Fifty Nine - Sylvia and Peter

Peter dies

It was to be the briefest and the saddest visit we had ever had from Sylvia

'No order today,' she said, 'just thought I should let you know Peter died on Monday. The funeral's on Friday if you can make it.'

I began to say how sorry I was which would not have been difficult, Peter being such a fine man. But Sylvia stopped me.

'Thank you, but it really was for the best. Friday then,' she said, telling me the time and the name of the church that was to hold the service. 'Lovely if you can make it,' she said with a convincing smile on her face as she left. Her walk upright and purposeful as she made her way along the road.

Arrangements to be made, no time to dally.

Sixty - The Old Rum Drinker

Wine drinkers and glasses

The old rum drinker came in today. He had under his arm a carrier bag, the contents of which I would hear about in due course.

'A quarter of dark rum,' he said, 'and two Special Brews.' He would usually buy the house rum even though he would never tire of telling you Woods Navy Rum was 'the finest rum in the whole world, the entire world in fact'.

As I wrapped the rum he opened his carrier bag.

'A wine drinker stole my glasses,' he said as he took something from the bag, 'and I've bought this book. Kirk Douglas I've followed his career for thirty years. Young Man Of Music was his best.'

He placed the rum and the Special Brews in the bag, followed by the book.

'A wine drinker,' he repeated, making it clear that this was a different thing from a rum drinker somehow.

'I'll no be able to see the print,' he said, bag and rum tucked firmly under his arm as he made to leave, 'and the landlord doesn't give a fuck. A right notorious character.'

Sixty One - Phillip

The remorseful drinker

'You saw me the other day, I know you did.'
This was Philip a local drinker, not yet a street drinker.
That was still to come. Quiet and harmless except perhaps
to himself.

'You saw me; I begged and took food from the bins. I
won't do that again, I let myself down.'

Philip was ashamed of what he had done, disgusted with
himself, 'Begging is wrong,' he continued, 'and eating
from bins? Better to starve or die of thirst than drink with
another man's money.'

At this moment he seemed close to tears or to rage. It was
difficult to know which.

'My father would have been ashamed, he would have
killed me.'

Philip was a man in his fifties now. Still governed, or
partly so at least, by his father's moral code.

'He would have killed me,' he said again, 'and I know that
you saw me.'

Sixty Two - The Students

Sausages and beer

The student had quickly realised that we specialised in rare beers from all over the world. Lagers from Russia or Zambia or other parts of Africa, powerful dark beers from Belguim with names like Demon, Grimbergon or Delierium Tremors. Beers from Australia such as Coopers sparkling ale or ales from micro-Breweries based in San Francisco. As we were not tied to any brewery, company or supplier, we were free to source beers from small sometimes unknown suppliers. We would stock them and advertise them on one of the blackboards situated outside the shop. Often someone would tell us they knew of this particular beer which they had encountered whilst travelling, or a friend had returned from their own travels with a bottle or two. Sometimes it was a way of reference for a customer to mention another beer from the same area that they particularly liked. If we stocked beers from one micro-brewery in San Francisco for instance, could we get hold of beers from another that they had come across in the area? Usually we could. This student, however, was not interested in beers from Africa or the west coast of America. This student was from Germany and was interested in certain beers from his country. Beers that went especially well with sausages. In particular, German beers to go with German sausages from a local delicatessen that he had in mind.

He was, he said planning a breakfast with friends. A breakfast of sausages and beer. The way they did things at home. He was instantly likeable and full of intelligence and of fun. Sometimes the two were not compatible.

I asked him to write down the names of the beers he would particularly like to accompany his breakfast with sausages. And as he wrote he spoke the characteristics of the beers, 'A dark wheat beer would be just right for the beef sausages,' he said as he wrote down the name, 'and something lighter, a Stein lager for the pork sausages,' and so on.

When I told him there would be no problem obtaining the beers and others beside, he looked for a second as though he were about to hug me. A fun intelligent hug. It seemed to me that while his planned breakfast was about good beer and company, it was also about something else, something more. A means for him to stay in touch with his homeland while he was away. A young man, a long way from home taking comfort in familiar things. And what could be more comforting than Beers and sausages. Perhaps after all that was worthy of a hug.

Sixty Three - Gary

Freddie Mercury

Gary was on particularly interesting form today. Full of purpose and brimming with life. His reply to, 'Morning Gary,' was a little richer than could reasonably have been expected in response to such a simple greeting. 'Serves him right for putting it up other blokes arses,' he said.

I assumed that Gary was referring to Freddie Mercury who had died the previous day.

'Everyone knows its AIDS,' he said, having made his own position perfectly clear on the sexuality and the cause of death of the much loved singer. 'Queer git,' he continued, to ensure there would be no doubt regarding this, 'great band though,' he added as he gathered his lunch trying to sing the Galileo segment from Bohemian Rhapsody as he did so. 'Everyone knows,' he said again, briefly interrupting his own singing.

No doubt at the factory this morning Freddie Mercury's death would have been all the workers were talking about around their machines, and over their tea and cigarettes. His death and his sexuality. Hopefully too, his music would be mentioned.

'Why hide it?' Gary continued as he took his coke from the cooler.

Perhaps Freddie Mercury's death had offered some kind of validation. Gary who lived with his parents and had never had a steady girlfriend. Or maybe it was just that Gary was homophobic or thought that he was.

'Great band though,' he said, 'I've got all his solo stuff too. Brilliant, best voice ever and what a performer live aid and that,' he said full of enthusiasm and admiration. Then remembering his stance on homosexuality adding, 'for a queer that is.'

Sixty Four - Adele

Adele sings a song

Adele seemed in good spirits today. A little flat lately, not uncommon for Adele, today though she was vivacious and cheerful. On good days, like this one, she would get caught up in the brightness of her mood, buoyed by something positive within her. On days such as this Adele would sing the words of an old song as she worked. Something heart breaking by Ella Fitzgerald or strong and affirmative such as Edith Piaf"s, *'Je ne regret'*. Some of it sang in the little French she remembered from childhood. The rest a hybrid of English and French with the occasional line from another song somehow finding its way into the lyrics.

I liked to hear Adele sing. It usually signified that she felt settled and well within herself. And things were ok for her, for now at least. Frank Sinatra had already had an airing, *'Something Stupid'* by way of Maria Callas was interesting and of course Edith would get in on the act so that the *'like I love you'* line from the song became almost operatic with a Gallic twist. Nice to hear her sing though and as off key as it was I would be happy to hear it every day.

As she sang she cleaned and polished the counter and wiped the bottles on the shelves.

There was one song that I never heard her finish. She would only sing the first line and then stop.

'Do Not Forsake Me Oh My Darling' is the song that appeared briefly but regularly in Adele's repertoire, summoned up it would seem from somewhere not of her choosing and without her consent. She would sing only that single solitary line then from being cheerful, at times even playful, she would stop, cease her singing and simply go silently about her work until the counter was clean and the bottles on the shelves about her pristine. Two customers had been served while Adele silently dusted and polished. Customers that she knew well but had failed to acknowledge or possibly even to recognise.

'Do Not Forsake Me Oh My Darling' was gone, for now anyway, and I never heard the next line sang by her though I knew it well enough. I knew also how often Adele had been forsaken by the French mother who had given her up for adoption, the mother that she would never meet. By the husband who cheated her out of her money and talked her out of motherhood, and by the friends that deserted her when the money was gone. And finally by the sister who lied and betrayed her throughout her life.

I switched on the radio. There would be no more singing this day and the silence needed to be filled.

Sixty Five - Ishmail

Serious Ishmail the second

Ishmail was refused again today. To her complete astonishment. She had walked in purposefully before looking around the place, as though for the first time. It was not long before she located the spirit section.

'That,' she said, pointing to a half bottle of Bells whisky, 'Just give it to me you eejit.'

Then began a stare, a long confused anxious stare. Something was coming to her and the expression on her face was that of a slow dawning.

'You're from hell,' she said at length. The expression of puzzlement being replaced by a look of fearful enlightenment.

'You' she said, everything in place now, 'you are the devil.'

She made the claim again louder now as she left the shop, almost running. A sideways crab like run which enabled her to keep her eyes fixed firmly upon me. Afraid that something evil may claim her if her gaze were to waiver.

'The devil,' she repeated before disappearing from sight, 'Bastard!'

Sixty Six - Sylvia and Peter

Funeral over

I had expected Sylvia to put on a brave face when next we saw her following Peter's funeral. For Sylvia, in public at least, there was no other way. The depth and intensity of her grief was a private thing. The funeral over now, with only a few exceptions the sadness of the mourning would remain within the boundaries of her home.

As she placed her order, reduced now, red wines and Spanish brandy would no longer be required, she chatted quite cheerfully.

'Went rather well I thought,' Sylvia said, referring to the funeral as she chose a couple of bottles of white wine. 'All done and dusted now,' she added. Then she paused for a moment in the selection of the wines, 'It really was for the best you know,' merriment gone for now replaced, I thought with a deep sincerity.

Some people say such things as a comfort, either for themselves or for the sake of others. I knew that if Sylvia said it then she would absolutely believe it. A kind woman, she was not taken to saying things she did not believe for the benefit of others. Never had been, why start now. Sylvia meant it though, entirely. Peter was suffering no longer and that meant everything to her. Her 'beautiful boy' was free now from his pain. She understood the significance of his passing and was aware of the logic of it too. Sylvia loved Peter and would rather lose him than see him that way any longer.

Sylvia placed the wines on the counter and asked if I thought she had made a good choice. She was familiar with the wines already, having bought them in the past but still I said yes she had. Perhaps she hadn't been referring to the wines at all. In either case the answer would have been the same.

Yes her choice had been good.

Her choice had been excellent.

Sixty Seven - The Drunks

Drunk C

Drunk C had been living rough for many years, but he didn't seem to be very good at it. He was always injured in some way. Cuts and bruises caused by falling over or by getting into fights. Broken fingers were a common occurrence as was damage to his face and in particular to his nose, which seemed as though it was permanently covered in new wounds. Deep cuts across the bridge or skin scraped from the flesh. New wounds to take their place amid the long established scar tissue.

He had been hospitalised many times, suffering from hypothermia in the winter, while in the summer months exposure to the sometimes baking sun would be the problem, falling drunkenly asleep in the full glare of the summer sunshine, awakening after many hours then often sleeping until the sun went down. Awaking burned and blistered and badly dehydrated. The blistering skin would often go untreated and the dehydration addressed by further drinking. A can of Special Brew to slate his thirst or a litre of Strongbow Cider, just to get him started again. This time, it being the heart of winter, his problem had been freezing temperatures.

Sober now in the store he carefully picked up a pack of lagers and brought them to the counter. Never a problem to us, we would serve him when sober and refuse when drunk. He always accepted the refusal without argument or aggression. He held the beers in his left hand, his right covered in bandages. Soaked through and black with mud and dirt. He was used to living rough and usually slept outdoors. Exposed to the elements whatever the time of year. The winter weather though, earlier in December, had been particularly harsh resulting in his becoming severely frost bitten.

He had, he told me quietly and without emotion, lost some toes and three fingers on his right hand. Also the thumb on that hand could not be saved.

Holding up the damaged hand he said, 'That's life eh?' before shrugging his shoulders and almost raising a smile. His extensive injuries no more than an occupational hazard or a small inconvenience. The use of a hand and the damage to his feet seen in the same way that another man would view a splinter from the garden or a nick from a razor.

Sixty Eight - Mrs Field

The fire

Mrs Field became quite a regular. Calling in everyday in fact. A whisky drinker in the main though not averse to wine on occasion, or gin in the warm weather. She was, I think always treated cordially, possibly over politely, in an attempt to compensate for any awkwardness our inexperience may have caused on her first visit to us. Mrs Field though had a character best described as changeable. On one day she could be pleasant, thoughtful, speaking of the weather or a programme she had watched on television the previous evening. Or make reference to something that had caught her attention in the morning papers. On another day she would be argumentative. Aggressively trying to pick a fight from nothing. Too many silver coins or copper coins in her change, music playing so loudly she could not hear herself think, or so quietly it seemed to her, that there was no point having music playing at all. On these occasions anything was fair game for a disagreement.

Often though she would be extremely kind. Bringing something with her as a gift for us. Flowers from her garden or a piece of cake she had baked herself. Sometimes a clipping from a magazine which she felt would be of interest. And it was not unknown for the kind Mrs Field to call in the morning, only to be replaced by the loud and aggressive Mrs Field later in the evening. 'Gordons,' she said today, this being a warm July evening 'three packets,' she added referring to the cigarettes she smoked.

We began to understand and read her moods, not responding or reacting to them. But knowing them all the same. And always attempting to serve her politely and efficiently. Quickly but not so quickly to suggest to her that she was being hurried from the shop. An action that would provoke anger and abuse from her.

I thanked her and smiled as I handed over her change. She didn't return the smile, I hadn't expected her too. And she neither thanked me, or cursed me which I considered a reasonable compromise. This was to be the last time she visited the shop. We were never to see her again.

In the early hours of the morning, Mrs Field, it was reported, had most probably fallen asleep whilst smoking in bed. Setting fire to the bedclothes, then the bed with her in it, empty gin bottles by her side.

The fire was eventually brought under control, the top two floors in the building all but destroyed and Mrs Field, Mrs Evelyn Field, gone with them, gone in an intoxicated stupor, drunk with the gin she had bought from us to accompany the cigarettes she had purchased that would kill her in her sleep.

Sixty Nine - Tess

Shelf-stacker extraordinaire

Tess was the baby whose life had once been threatened by a drunk. He had been aggressive and demanding in pursuit of more alcohol. Another can of lager.

'I'll put burning rags through the letter box when everyone is sleeping,' he had said.

A lovely baby then, a delightful teenager now and spending weekends with me, her mother and I having separated when she was a year old. It was a Sunday, and on a Sunday she would help in the shop. Becoming for the day the shelf-stacker.

She would take great pride in the stocking of the confectionary units. Sometimes rearranging them so that her particular favourites took pride of place. Also she would help draw up the next order of sweets and chocolates. Often suggesting weird and wonderful things that usually a wine store would not stock; flying saucers, pink shrimps, sherbet dips and the like. Students, somewhere between childhood themselves and adulthood loved them. Loving the novelty and still young enough to be in touch with their childlike senses to love the taste. She would remain quite childlike herself as she went about her work, smiling and chatting. An impromptu dance being performed from time to time. A frown too, occasionally, when trying to concentrate hard to pinpoint the next great range of confectionary that a store must stock. This would change though quite suddenly when a handsome young student or a good looking local teenager came in. Then she would become, though only briefly, shy and awkward and silent. Ever changing, ever special. When Tess was in the shop it was no longer work. Now it had become one of life's great pleasures and spent in the company of a lovely and fascinating young lady. When the handsome student had left, the wine shelves received her attention. Then the snacks, crisps and nuts some tidied and rearranged. Then it would be time for the spirits or more particularly the miniatures which were stored in a large mixed box waiting to restock the shelves.

Tess liked stocking the miniatures, tiny versions of the full bottles we stocked. She thought they were 'cute'. It was some years later that I found out, from her future husband, that Tess considered the tiny vodkas the cutest of all. Cute and handbag size, perfectly fitting into the handbag, perfect too for a night out.

A good well behaved loving daughter, the temptation must have been overwhelming. No longer simply a kid in a sweet store now a teenager in a liquor store. And the new and irresistible candy was vodka in miniature. Her teenage years would pass and we would live with the minor short lived losses.

One day she would become a fine wife and a wonderful mother. That time was not really that far away.

For now though she would help her daddy in the wine store. And dance and chat.

Shelf stacker extraordinaire. Extraordinary daughter too.

Seventy - The Complainers

Mr W and his wine

Mr W rushed through the door as though being chased by a fierce dog.

'This wine is off,' he said banging an empty bottle of Brouilly on the counter and, 'I have dinner guests waiting.' Wine can be off for many reasons. A badly fitting or dried out cork, poor storage, exposure to extreme heat or intense cold amongst others. Mostly the problem lies though with the cork. If the cork is too dry it ceases to keep the bottle airtight. And exposure to air will adversely affect any wine, very quickly. Some times in a restaurant perhaps a wine will be sent back for having a tiny piece of cork floating in it. And this wine is often referred to as being corked. But it isn't. A speck or two of random pieces of cork is not a problem. Corked wine is wine that has been exposed to air by a badly fitting cork. It's a random situation, an occasional misfortune, and can effect wines from a cooperative in Australia to the great Chateaux of Bordeaux.

'It's corked' said Mr W looking a little angrier I thought than the occasion demanded.

Normally if a wine is returned we will replace it automatically either with another bottle of the same or of something else of a similar value. The representative of the company we purchased the wine from will, understanding the situation regarding the occasional spoiled wine will issue a credit for it. So, very little harm done. For the rep to do this however, there needs to be wine in the bottle for him to issue the credit. This bottle was empty.

I pointed this out to Mr. W explaining there was no wine to be returned as it had apparently been consumed. Still though Mr W would have had his replacement if he had managed not to bang the empty bottle on the counter for the 3rd or 4th time and bellow,

'Of course we drank it. We didn't realise at first you idiot. It was foul.'

For the sake of customer relations I had been about to back down and ask him to choose another wine and say to him that I hoped he could still enjoy his evening. Instead I simply said we would not be replacing the wine. His empty bottle of wine.

Red faced he turned on his heel after abusing the shop and the wines and then myself personally. I wasn't too pleased with myself, I felt I had handled the situation badly. I felt we both had.

Before clearing away the empty bottle I poured the tiny amount left in to a glass, sniffed it, held it up to the light and finally tasted it. Which is in fact what I should have done earlier. And though it certainly wasn't 'foul' as Mr W. had claimed it to be, still it could have been in better condition.

Without the bellowing and the banging Mr W. would have had his wine and I would have kept a customer. His guests would not have gone thirsty and I might not have been labeled 'an idiot'.

Seventy One - Gary

The NHS

'Fucking N.H.S.' said Gary as he took his coke from the cooler, 'needs a good kicking. This old girl,' he continued, picking up crisps and chocolate bars as he spoke, 'friend of my mum's needs an operation. Something wrong with her eyes. Fucking cataracts,' he said after a short pause to ensure he had the right medical terminology.

'Never leaves the house, nearly blind. Scared she'll fall over, or get hit by a bus.'

Gary seemed to have an innate fear of buses which he shared with his mother's friend.

'An English old girl, lived here all her life, and blind now,' he added, rapidly worsening her cataract condition. Gary had mentioned before the unfairness of paying tax for foreigners to come to England for 'free operations' or to give birth.

'Six months she's got to wait stumbling about in the dark this old girl. Its shit!' he said, appearing to have finished now, though he wasn't, not quite.

'Did a good job on my back though, after they fished me out of the canal.'

Gary rubbed his back subconsciously as he recalled the accident. The fork-lift truck, which he operated at work had fallen into the water with him on board.

'No barriers or nothing,' he reminded me.

'Still plays me up though,' he said, remembering there was a court case regarding settlement pending, 'like a cripple some days. And the old girl's almost blind with her cataracts and a bus with her number on it heading her way. Six months,' he said earnestly as he left the shop to return to work, 'not right to make a blind old girl wait that long. Not right at all.'

Seventy Two - Radiohead

Just a local band

Radiohead had a fantastic and powerful presence on stage. Their lead singer possessing an incredible voice and song writing talent to match the grace and wonder of his voice. Around that time Oxford was something of a breeding ground for bands, some like, Ride, would make it, others such as, The Candyskins and, The Jennifers, though possessing equal or greater musical talent, sadly would not. Many years later, beyond the confines of this book, it would be referred to as the X Factor. An often intangible quality almost impossible to define. Some had it, to a certain degree while others had this quality in abundance. Radiohead were one such band and would go on to be, for a while, one of the biggest and most admired bands in the world.

In the shop two people were quietly going about the business of choosing wine. One of them I did not recognise the other I did. It was Thom Yorke, lead singer of Radiohead.

I had seen them play locally two or three times before they were to become a world phenomenon and considered them a good though not great band. Badly misjudging their talent.

Thom Yorke and his friend brought three bottles of medium priced wines to the counter and began looking at the vodkas. Stolichnaya they both liked and asked for two bottles. Also Grey Goose was good, so a bottle of that was added.

Thom Yorke was quiet and unassuming at that time, off stage at least. Some years later after the huge success that happened he still sometimes came in. His child with him now and cozy in his buggy. Still he was the same and seemed to exhibit no ego and no arrogance. I thought him incredibly modest regarding his fame.

A female student approached him one time as he paid for his drinks. The out of context element, not recognising your dentist in a restaurant, came into play. She had smiled at him and in a friendly manner said,'I'm sure I know you from somewhere,' genuinely puzzled, adding 'you look so familiar.'

He didn't reply, as others may have with, 'I'm the lead singer of a hugely successful band, and writer of beautiful and innovative songs, in possession of one of the finest voices ever to grace popular music.' He simply replied, 'I can't place it either but you look familiar too. Oh well,' he said shrugging his shoulders and manoeuvring the child and buggy. 'Enjoy your wine,' he added as he moved from the counter.

'You too,' she said, still puzzled as he left the shop. Perhaps many things must combine to create that undefined quality, later to be called the X factor. Modesty combined with great talent and humility may, just be a few of them. Thom Yorke had these in abundance and I suspect a few more besides.

Seventy Three - The Yorkshire Gentleman

Feeling unwell

The Yorkshire gentleman hadn't called in for some time. Usually he would visit every two or three days for his cans of Heineken. But recently, he said, after his polite good morning, he had been a 'bit under the weather'.

'Quite poorly in fact,' he added.

There had been a nasty bug doing the rounds, Influenza racked customers would come in for whisky for hot toddies or brandy to comfort them and to help them to sleep. They would cough and sneeze and share their germs in the short time it took to complete the transaction. Sometimes they would mention as they asked for Benson and Hedges and Marlboro lights that they could barely manage the walk to the shops and that it was all that they could do to even draw breath at all.

The Yorkshire gentleman told me he hadn't been out of the house for two weeks, spending most of his time in bed trying to read, or on the sofa watching TV.

'Haven't touched a drop of this stuff for a fortnight,' he had said, tapping the cans of lager that he had placed on the counter.

'Most unpleasant,' he said referring to the illness rather than the beer, 'and dull too, stuck on your own for all that time.'

I knew from his expression that there was more to come,

something he needed to add. I'd seen him with that look before. A distant gaze as though attempting to focus on something a little too far off, almost slipping beyond his vision. But something that he refused to let go of and would never allow himself not to see.

'She would have made me soup,' he said, referring to his wife, 'and offered a word or two of comfort, I shouldn't doubt. Always made me up a bed on the sofa. A proper bed mind, with sheets and pillows.'

He had grasped the thing now that for a moment had seemed so far away. Now he had it and had no intention of releasing it from his grasp.

'It almost made being unwell a pleasure, all the attention, all the fuss. Anyway I'm well now, that's the main thing.'

He placed the cans in his bag and paid me for them.

'Chicken soup it would have been, with pearl barley,' he said as he left the shop.

His eyes red from the virus and moist from memories that he would never permit to leave or allow even, to fade.

Seventy Four - Gary

Gary and the eight grand

Gary had an accident at work some time back. Gary works at Lucy's factory, an old and failing workplace awaiting demolition. Barely updated since Victorian times, the machinery is antiquated and the building itself resembles a Dickensian workhouse.

They have a modern fork lift truck though and Gary is its driver.

'Offered me eight grand the fuckers,' he said by way of a greeting, 'eight grand. Fucked me back up and I'm still getting dizzy spells. Told them where to put it, should be a hundred grand that's what we asked for.'

Gary's fork lift had ended up in the canal with him on board 'I could have been dead. That's an insult that is; eight grand out of court. Is that all I'm worth. I can hardly work some days, worse when it rains. I told them to piss off. A hundred grand,' he continued, 'that's fair.'

When he gets his money, the hundred grand that is his due, he's going to 'piss off' to Greece or somewhere. Get out of this country, too many foreigners. Greece would be 'all right'. He went there once 'miserable fuckers though the Greeks and shit food and no sweet wine at all'.

Seventy Five - The Complainers

Mrs F and her sherry

Some people have the ability to make your heart drop even before they have spoken a word. Almost never having the desire or in fact seeing the point in beginning any encounter on a positive note. They begin with a negative and continue downwards from there. Mrs F was one such person and she was about to enter the shop.

'I am not at all enamoured with this,' she said removing a half empty bottle of Harvey's Luncheon Dry from her bag and placing it on the counter, 'tastes completely different these days. It should be dry. Where is the dryness?' she said pointing an angry, slightly shaky finger at the offending bottle.

It was difficult to tell if it was her annoyance making the finger shake or more to do with the sherry that was absent from the bottle.

'Not nice,' she said 'not nice at all.'

In an attempt to explain and possibly to calm her I suggested that from time to time products, wines, sherries most things really, vary a little. Grapes varying, even if only slightly from one harvest to the next. Quality can vary slightly and taste too sometimes, in a very small way altered. I could see she had begun to lose interest and was in addition probably annoyed that her complaint was not given free rein to build speed and urgency as it gathered momentum. Also, I said hopefully people's tastes in general change over time, leaning more towards a drier wine perhaps or a fuller slightly sweeter sherry. Or Mars bars or coca-cola I wanted to say but thought better of it. Sometimes a product might be tinkered with I added hopefully.

'Tinkered with!' she said, the finger being pointed at me now giving the sherry bottle a welcome break, 'tinkered with. It has been totally adulterated, ruined, bastardised,' she finished with, capping herself and for some reason surprising me also.

I kept quiet now after my poor attempt at an explanation, reasoning that saying nothing was better than risking another 'tinkered with'. Though the word 'tweeked' did briefly cross my mind.

'Well?' she asked 'well then,' she said again having received no response from me.

'Why do you still stock it?'

'It's very popular,' was all I could come up with.

'Do you then stock a sherry that is dry dry, properly dry?' she said sharply, 'the way Luncheon Dry used to be. Not dryish or off dry or medium, which is in fact sweet to anyone with a reasonably defined palate.'

She settled finally on a Tio Pepe, having been assured of its unwavering dryness.

'I hope this one has not been tinkered with,' she said, pleased with herself as she paid and made to leave the store, 'or I shall return it,' she added on her way out off of the door, 'rest assured.'

As I began to serve the next customer, a simple transaction of two bottles of Australian Shiraz, I made a mental note. Do not use the words 'tinkered with' or heaven forbid 'tweeked' ever again. Words like that carelessly banded about could start a riot if not a full scale war.

Seventy Six - The Quiet Nurse

Adele

Adele was often positioned behind the counter dusting the spirit shelves or stocking the cigarette display unit. Therefore it would often be Adele who would answer the phone. Her voice always throaty and her tone unintentionally harsh. She would unnerve customers and disturb friends seeming to bark the name of the store into the telephone as she raised it to her ear. And for an old lady she was quick. If she was in a position three of four feet closer to the phone than anyone else it was hers. No matter how many times she would be asked to leave it for someone else. If she was close to it, she would claim it. Hers to pick up and rasp into, hers to bewilder a potential customer on the line, hers to confuse the gender of the caller often calling men, madam, and women, sir.

It was hers also on occasion to vet personal calls.

'No I am afraid he is busy now,' I heard her say into the mouthpiece. Probably due to her background, her history, Adele could be overprotective about things and more particularly about the people she cared for. At times this would manifest as possessiveness. Adele had lost so many people one way or another throughout her life, she would do all that she could to keep hold of the few that still remained.

I asked Adele who was calling only to hear her say, 'Yes of course I can take a message,' though she made no move to pick up a pen to write the message on the notepad needed to record it in.

'I'll take it Adele,' I said, trying to pitch my tone so it would leave no room for debate.

'He's available now,' she said, handing me the telephone and resuming her work with the cigarettes.

'Is that you?' asked the familiar voice on the end of the line.

'It is now,' I answered.

'It's not easy is it?' she said, referring to getting past Adele and I could hear amusement in her voice. We spoke warmly and comfortably for a few minutes. I felt excited to be speaking to her and I could feel my heart racing. Adele gave me a look as she heard me suggest the place for our next date. It was to be an Italian restaurant, my suggestion this time. Somewhere I knew we would have a good time but then we always seemed to have a good time. And there was not too much that Adele could do about that.

The call finished, I approached Adele and gave her a hug. It was as always like hugging the thin trunk of an ancient tree, though I knew she was smiling.

I was aware of something very powerful happening to me regarding the shy nurse, feelings so strong. Elation, excitement and great attraction. And I missed her when I did not see her. I had no way of knowing where it would go with her or whether it would develop and last. I knew that I wanted it to, but all the same Adele had no need to worry. Nothing would change how I felt for that overprotective, vulnerable old lady. You don't lose people you love. The hug completed we went quietly back to work and I started thinking about Friday.

Seventy Seven - Ann Andrews

The intrepid drinker

Anne Andrews had inadvertently presented us with a dilemma. Marched into the shop by her husband who, I felt to her great embarrassment, had asked us to stop selling alcohol to his wife.

Mrs. Andrews had been buying bottles of spirits from us for some years now. Mrs. Andrews was in her early forties, a typical married, middle class housewife.

His voice was raised as he insisted we 'desist' from 'providing' his wife with alcohol.

Mrs. Andrews was asked if she was in agreement with this request. She nodded and looked at the floor. A naughty school girl, though it must be said a school girl who had made a serious dent in the contents of her parents' drinks cabinet. We agreed that yes if that was what they both wanted, then of course we would do this.

'Thank you,' he said, before escorting his wife from the premises.

Over the weeks that followed, I had noticed Mrs. Andrews getting on buses looking inebriated. Getting off buses and looking more inebriated still. I noticed her coming and goings far more than was usual to do, so anxious was I that she would enter the shop one day to order a bottle of vodka or a litre of gin.

I would see her walking back from the centre of town on returning from its suburbs. Never once did she look sober. Never once did I see her smile. One Monday morning she abandoned her bus trip and a walk into the town.

'Two bottles of Smirnoff please,' she said, her voice already slurred at 10.30am, 'and some lemonade.'
I reminded Mrs. Andrews of the visit accompanied by her husband. The request they had made and the answer that they had been given. Mrs. Andrews didn't argue or disagree. She simply left the shop. There were other places no doubt where she could purchase her vodka. It was unlikely that her husband had marched her into every shop and pub in town. However well intentioned he had been in his attempt to curtail his wife's supply, there would always be somewhere his wife would be served. It was impossible to call on them all.

Seventy Eight - Sylvia and Peter

The brandy

Sylvia had said at the time of Peter's death that it was for the best and that it was better that way. I believed her, I always believed Sylvia. She never says anything simply for effect or that she doesn't feel to be true. She simply wouldn't see the point of that. Sylvia still called into the shop regularly though her order was different now. Her 'good morning' was always upbeat and today was no different. Cheery in a natural unforced way.

'Have you any Ame' or Aqua Libra?' she asked, 'and twelve bottles of white wine, you choose.'

It had been some six months now since Peter had died and I suspect I was not alone in that when I saw Sylvia I still half expected to see Peter and he would always come to mind. I told Sylvia that we had Ame' in stock and suggested as the weather was warm, Orvieto or Frascati Superiore for the wine.

'Splendid,' she replied, 'sounds just right.'

Sylvia rarely ordered Shiraz or Cabernet Sauvignon anymore. It had been Peter who favoured red wine or a glass of Metaxa or Fundador brandy. Perhaps the brandy had eased his discomfort in later years or perhaps he simply enjoyed a glass of Greek or Spanish brandy. Today though Sylvia added red wine and Fundador brandy to her order, 'for later,' she said by way of explanation.

We would always chat for a few minutes while Sylvia was in the shop. I would offer a stool to take the weight off her feet. Physically strong, robust even, still Sylvia would sometimes be a little weary if her visit to us coincided with a trip into town. Sylvia would always walk into the town centre. Sylvia seemed to walk everywhere. Today she refused the stool as she had things to do at home and did not intend to stay too long. She would ask about Adele if Adele was not in the shop and enquire as to her health. And she would offer a bit of, what in other hands, would be considered gossip. But from Sylvia it came over more as high class information, relevant and necessary to know. We would sometimes talk briefly about politics especially if there was a local election coming up. Local issues and local politics were important to Sylvia. At some point I would usually ask her how she was, meaning it to be in a general way and usually she would respond as such. Today there was a delay, before she said, 'It is Peter's birthday today and we are having some people round.' Sylvia finally sat on the stool I had offered her.

'A cause for celebration don't you think? If it wasn't for this day we would never have known him, and his favourite brandy is for the toast.'

Sylvia looked convincing as though she meant it, positive and upbeat and in the mood for a celebration. And as untroubled as a person could be having lost the love of her life.

Seventy Nine - Gary

Frustrated about the settlement

Gary's patience over his settlement was being sorely tried. He would tell you that himself.

'Sodding sick of it,' he said, picking up a bottle of Coke, 'Tight sods.' Gary was holding out for the hundred thousand that his solicitor had assured him was his due. 'This is the worst,' he said, pointing outside at the rain, 'cripples me like an old man of fifty.'

Gary gathered his crisps and chocolate bars in an animated fashion, angry and annoyed with the Mars bars and the Twix, and seemingly furious with the Coke Cola that he banged on the counter. His lunch gathered he still had a point to make.

'They think I'm an idiot,' he said, shaking his head in disbelief, astonished that they could so misjudge him. 'They think I'll get sick of it and take whatever they offer me. They can sod off,' he added by way of stating his determination to see it through to the bitter end, 'no way forget it. They won't even return my solicitor's calls now. Just ignorant twats,' he added, clearing up any loose ends.

Then he was gone to do battle with his lunch and to simmer away another afternoon in the factory. The place that had ruined his health ancient and crumbling and run by men 'too ignorant' to communicate and 'too mean' to make a decent settlement for the accident that had almost crippled him and had made him feel like an old man of fifty.

Eighty - The Drunks

Drunk D and Drunk E

As was sometimes the case it was street drinkers that were to be our first customers of the day. A fairly affluent area most of our local customers were out working, intent on obtaining the means to maintain their affluent lifestyles. But still the street drinkers would find their way here, and they had nothing as mundane as work to distract them from their main business. That of obtaining and consuming alcohol.

'Where do you keep the brew?' Drunk D asked, referring to Carlsberg Special Brew.

Both men were reasonably clean and sober having not yet began the days drinking in a determined way. I had never seen either of them before. But as long as they were reasonably polite and not drunk or aggressive then they would be served. It seemed unfair and possibly prejudiced to do otherwise. I answered Drunk D telling him that we did not sell Special Brew or any of the super strength lagers.

'No brew?' he said shaking his head, unable or unwilling to believe it. 'No brew?' he said again, perplexed now. Many street drinkers and many alcoholics would personalise a drink making it sound more familiar, more common place and nothing out of the ordinary. Woods One Hundred Per Cent Navy Rum would become Woodseys. Special Brew would be referred to simply as brew. Making it sound almost both healthy and wholesome more like a cup of tea than a super strong lager that most people would struggle to finish one can of. Tennant's Super would become Super T, almost transforming it into a health drink. Thunderbird, a fierce, rough wine of some twenty percent alcohol strength would be shortened to T-Bird. A fun harmless sounding name like a character from a cartoon or a children's book. Sherry was usually referred to simply as wine. If a street drinker asked for dry wine or sweet wine he was not intending to buy Muscadet or Sauternes, he was asking for sherry. Simply port was port wine. Innocuous sounding names customised and made innocent, and what then could be the harm in that.

They made friends of their particular drink and like all friends they would sometimes disagree. Or having slowly moved in different directions for so long they would find themselves falling out more and more until it became clear that in fact they no longer got along at all.

'What have you got then?' asked Drunk D.

I told him Stella was the strongest lager stocked.

'Stella,' he said forming a habit of repeating the word or words I had just said.

'Gnats piss,' said Drunk E, giving me the critical benefit of his experience.

'Two bottles of medium wine then,' Drunk D said, pointing to the Sherries, 'the cheapest you have.'

And though the chcapest we had was still far too expensive in their opinion they bought them all the same.

'No brew or Super T,' said Drunk D as they made to leave the shop, not pleased with their purchases or the price they had paid, 'no brew or cheap wine, what a dump, 'he said loud enough for me to hear. Not quite so polite now.

'Shit hole,' added his friend as they left the shop, 'a right shit hole.'

Eighty One - Gary

Gazumping

'Fucking gazumping,' said Gary sounding like an X-rated version of Batman.

'My neighbour, an old girl had a heart attack over it.' Gary had driven to work today on account of the weather being 'fucked'. He usually travelled the three miles or so to the factory by moped.

'Not today though,' he said in response to my good morning, 'In this?' he said indicating the weather that no one but himself had mentioned, 'no way, you must be joking. Forget it get blown under a bus or a lorry, just to get to that place. They'd love that wouldn't they?' he said , referring to the fact that they owed him money for his accident.

'These people came round,' he said, returning to his original theme, 'we'll give you fifteen grand less. She thought it was all done, the old girl, fifteen grand or you can keep it.'

Gary thought they were 'cheeky sods' and said as much. 'Now she can't afford to buy a new place. And she's still got to pay for the survey and the solicitors. Fifteen grand or we don't want it. Sods' he said, abbreviating his assessment, 'she's in hospital now. Nearly died. Gazumping shouldn't be allowed, nearly killed her, the bastards.'

Gary left and got into his car. A red three wheeler, to drive around the corner, to begin his day's work. The car door stuck as he tried to open it which seemed to annoy him.

Maybe it wasn't this though that irritated him, the car door sticking, maybe it was the gazumpers, or the unfairness of a world that allowed such a thing to happen. Or perhaps it was simply the weather. The callous, cruel, heartless weather that would have blown him under a bus or a lorry, if he hadn't had the presence of mind to leave his moped at home.

Eighty Two - Adele

Adele wants to quit

It was one of Adele's days off and she called into see us. She was not looking to buy Guinness today, and her head was clear, not swirling from her medication mixed with beer. This day her mind was sharp but in her eyes there was a sadness. Adele had called to resign. She had not wanted to waste actual work time with this announcement. She was paid for that time and this was a private thing, a personal thing so then it should be on her time not ours.

Adele was prone to bouts of depression and the occasional psychotic episode. She had resigned before a few years back only to spend too much time at home often on her own. We would visit her as would certain other friends but still sometimes for days on end she would see no one. The only voices she would hear would be that of the television newsreaders or radio presenters. Some days she would not hear even those disembodied voices, preferring to sit and look at a blank TV screen or to stay in bed, an unread book lying on her lap.

'I can't do it any longer my dear,'she said, her eyes hardened now. Commitment rather than tears, sadness temporarily at least, replaced by determination. At various times since her first resignation, Adele had been talked out of leaving but this time it was right to listen to her.

'I'm seventy-four now and not doing things as well as I should like.'

To Adele doing things to the best of your ability was not enough. Things should be done properly and well. To Adele receiving money for a job done under par was not acceptable. It would be akin to stealing or at least receiving money under false pretences. This time there would be no talking her out of it. We embraced, the stiff tentative embrace of someone who had not had a child or known the love of a parent. A bony, awkward embrace. With Adele there was no other. The announcement made, the brittle hug complete, she left the shop. Her working life over.

'I am sorry my dear,' she said as she left, 'I am so sorry.' Adele had no reason to say that, no reason to be sorry for anything, no reason whatsoever.

Eighty Three - Gary

Gary gets his settlement

'Had to do it didn't they?' Gary asked as he came in, 'Ninety grand.'

Gary had received his settlement for his damaged back. 'Supposed to be a hundred' he added clearly annoyed that he had been short changed. Though, 'I'm pissed off' was the way he put it.

'Couldn't do the right thing could they?' he said, seemingly talking to the Kettle Chips he was in the process of choosing. He went on to elaborate on his grievance, saying how unfair it was that they couldn't give the proper amount due, to a man needlessly damaged in the work place.

'Wouldn't have killed them,' he said reasonably enough. Gary had been making plans for the money for as long as I could remember. He was buying a new car on Monday, 'Something with four wheels this time, a Ford or a Vauxhall,' he said placing Ritter chocolate, Kettle Chips and Cashew nuts on the counter.

Gary's lunch was to be decidedly up-market today.

'And I will be buying something for my mum.'

There was always Gary's mum.

'Can't go abroad now,' he said reading my mind, 'It would kill the old girl. Die of a broken heart or something even worse'. Gary was never one to underestimate the influence he had on his mother or her health.

'It would kill her' he said, leaving it unclear if her death would be due to her broken heart or whether it was the, 'something worse that got her.'

He went on to further explain why he would not be leaving his parent's home.

'Nowhere I fancy that much anyway,' he said, 'it's not so bad here.'

He was planning to visit Thailand though and taking a month off.

'Sod 'em' he suggested, referring to the factory bosses, 'Can't sack me now can they? How would that look?'

I wondered as I watched him if the money, his new found wealth would change him. And though I rarely agreed with his opinions or much of what he said, still I found myself hoping that it wouldn't. He may be wrong about so many things, though right and wrong is often a matter of opinion but he was, in his own way straight forward, open and honest.

And in spite of his sometimes dubious views some of which I felt he may have picked up in childhood, and had yet to lose, I believed that he was fundamentally, a decent man.

'Thailand,' he said, immediately testing my overall opinion of him, 'the blokes say it's great. Hot and cheap and women everywhere. Have to be careful though, some of them are not women at all. They just look like women. Have to keep an eye out for them especially on the lash.'

Gary paid me for his lunch and put his things in a carrier bag.

'What's that about eh?' he asked leaving the shop, to count his money, to treat his mum and to make plans for Thailand, 'Lady boys what's that about?' he said again. Then after a pause in which I assumed he was using to attempt to answer his own question he came to a conclusion.

'Queer fuckers,' he said happy now with his assessment, and Gary knew about homosexuals. 'must be' he added as he walked to the door, 'their lives though, up to them.'

A new found streak of liberalism seeming to have arrived with his ninety thousand pounds.

'If they want to be queer fuckers that is.'

And then without looking back, Gary reached the door and he was gone.

Eighty Four - Adele

Adele shuts down

Adele shut down today, less than two weeks after her resignation, ten days in fact. She couldn't call in to give us the news directly; a policeman did that on her behalf.

'She hadn't seemed to have suffered,' he said, meaning well though knowing little of her life.

Gone then, finally gone and no doubt her stockpile of painkillers and sleeping tablets gone too. She would know me at this moment and no doubt pull my leg. She would tell me I was 'a fart in a trance' or a 'willow the wisp.' I never truly understood what she meant, though I think I got the main gist of it.

A second mother for me, perhaps for Adele a first son. If life so often had seemed beyond her control then death at least had been this way. A time of her choosing and the circumstances. In her home, in her bed, not a care home or hospital bed. Her choice, finally now for once, her choice.

Eighty Five

This is the end

Mr and Mrs Singh will arrive soon to collect the keys, and the shop and the building which houses it will belong to them. Never closed except for Christmas Day, this morning it is closed. Always subdued the store when out of working hours. Today though it seemed to me a solemn place. A new cycle was about to begin for it too, and the shop was entitled to a moment's rest to draw breath in readiness to start anew.

A few customers invisible behind the window blind had tried the door, surprised no doubt to see the door locked during normal opening hours. I felt surprise too and elation and sadness and though moving on was what I wanted I was experiencing a sense of loss.

A happy place the shop, for the most part happy I think. The choosing of wine or beers or champagne should be a pleasant undertaking. The thought of drinking the wine in good company over a pleasant meal, or the beer in the sunshine or Champagne to celebrate an anniversary or the birth of a child or graduating from university.

The shop is silent. There is usually music to accompany the comings and goings of people. Today music somehow feels inappropriate. Mostly happy the shop, though occasionally while looking for drink one or two would seek confrontation or look for a fight or an argument. For many like Sylvia and Peter a trip to the wine store was just one of many roads to fun, and when they called they brought love here. They carried it with them at all times.

Sylvia and Peter understood and respected love. Most of all they upheld it and sustained it.

The students sometimes devalued love believing it to be easily acquired and constantly attainable. Abundant in supply, inexhaustible and therefore without great worth. Gary loves his mum and Freddie Mercury in spite of Freddie's sexuality, Dennis loved his job and was broken when it left him. Charlie loved not being a pub landlord. Adele mistrusted love, having been tricked and cheated in love, she learned how to get by without it, surviving if not flourishing. Pauline played love so close to her chest that in time it burned out her heart. The Yorkshire gentleman absorbed love so it became a part of his DNA keeping his love for his wife alive, involving her in all that he did and all that he is. The drunks traded love exchanging it for an extra drink and then another to take its place. Sometimes aware they had squandered and neglected love and resentful of that, resentful of many things but mostly of themselves, for letting a good woman go, for letting a good woman slip away.

 Drunk X had once said, in the way that street drinkers can often be profound in their drinking, 'If you've got a good woman you should cherish her. I had a good woman once, I didn't look after her. I went with other women. They had nothing on her.'

The quiet nurse, who is not so shy trusts to love, believing that to be enough. She will not be squandered or traded, she will be cherished.

'If you have a good woman you should cherish her' and I will drink to that.

Sloncha!

Nabros Ka!

Stin Yamas!

Cheers!